shoptalk

shoptalk

learning to write
with writers

donald m. murray

BOYNTON/COOK PUBLISHERS
HEINEMANN
Portsmouth, NH

BOYNTON/COOK PUBLISHERS
A Division of
HEINEMANN EDUCATIONAL BOOKS, INC.
361 Hanover Street, Portsmouth, NH 03801
Offices and agents throughout the world

"At 64, Talking without Words." From *Poetry* 155 (March 1990). Copyright © 1990 by The Modern Poetry Association; reprinted by permission of the Editor of *Poetry*.

"Waiting for a Poem." From *Poetry* 153 (March 1989). Copyright © 1989 by The Modern Poetry Association; reprinted by permission of the Editor of *Poetry*.

Library of Congress Cataloging-in-Publication Data
Murray, Donald Morison, 1924–
    Shoptalk : learning to write with writers / Donald M. Murray.
      p. cm.
    Includes bibliographical references.
    ISBN 0-86709-258-0
    1. Authorship–Quotations, maxims, etc.   2. Authors–Quotations.
  I. Title.
PN165.M8   1990
808'.02–dc20   89-77216
                                                    CIP

Front-cover photo by Trish Harrington.
Back-cover photo by Gary Samson, University of New Hampshire.
Designed by Wladislaw Finne.
Printed in the United States of America.
92 93 94 10 9 8 7 6 5 4 3 2

for Chip Scanlan

a fine writer and a supportive friend
who has been a patient companion in my explorations
of the writer's craft

contents

acknowledgments

Through the many years it has taken to develop, organize, and computerize this collection, I have had the support, first of all, of my wife Minnie Mae, who has typed many of the quotations. When I worked with Burton Albert, Jr., on a project for *Reader's Digest,* he made important contributions to the collection, collation, and reproduction of the quotations. The University of New Hampshire has supported this collection with a grant, and Professor Donald H. Graves has understood this obsession of mine, as he has most of my others. Susan Sowers, Mary Peterson, Ginger Reynolds, and Elaine Messier have given me valuable assistance in recording and organizing the collection. And Toby Gordon, Nancy Sheridan, and others at Heinemann—Boynton/Cook have helped to see and execute this book; credit them for what you like and the author for what you don't.

I also want to express my appreciation to Dr. Barbara Tomlinson of the University of California at San Diego, who has done important work in this field, and to Ann Vibert, who has helped me see the scholarly significance of what writers say about writing.

preface

what writers know

This book began when I was in junior high school. I'd ride the trolley or, if I was out of sight of home, thumb my way from North Quincy, Massachusetts, down Hancock Street to Quincy Square and the huge main library. There I would wander through the open stacks, discovering new authors and new worlds of knowledge. School was boring but never these tall canyons of books.

One day I came upon a book by Burton Rascoe, who talked about the writer's world and the writer's life. I was fascinated by a life I might live; but more than that, brought up on the legends of King Arthur, I thought that reading about writing might reveal the magic secret of composition. I would be able to free the sword from the stone and become a great writer.

I started taking home books on writing and collecting quotations from writers about their craft, beginning a commonplace book more than a decade before I knew the term. I never discovered the secret that allowed some to tug the sword free of the stone without effort, but I never lost my fascination with what writers said about writing.

I have continued to collect quotations by writers ever since. My collection, a page or more to a quotation, filled twenty-four three-inch-thick notebooks at one time, at least eight thousand quotations, that I winnowed down to about twelve hundred to put on the computer. And that collection has grown back to at least three thousand.

This was no scholarly enterprise. I had been promoted to junior high by an elementary school principal who said, "We don't want you around here anymore." I doubted if I would finish high school and, in fact, I was to drop out of North Quincy High twice before flunking out. I didn't know about footnotes, proper scholarly references; I just wanted to know how writers wrote. I have references for most of these quotations but they are often sketchy, uneven, and, possibly, although I have made efforts to see this is not true, inaccurate. I hope appropriately trained scholars will take up this work and do what I have not done with true scholarly discipline.

From the beginning I delighted in contradiction, in fact sought more than I found. I have always been comfortable with dissonance from teachers, bosses, ministers, sergeants, colleagues. This book has some strong consistencies, but I hope you will find striking differences among authors and even, at times, in what a writer says at different times.

Now, more than fifty years after I first explored the low 800 numbers of the Dewey Decimal System in the main library of the Quincy Public Library, I have selected my favorite quotations to share with you. The strength and weakness of this book is the same: it is an eccentric, personal collection. The quotations were not selected originally for publication, but for personal need. These quotations were what I needed to hear. If my writer friends were to read the same sources they would probably choose quite different selections. I make no apology for this. I delight in these quotations; I hope you will as well.

I have organized them into sixteen categories and ordered them into a sequence that makes sense to me. The quotations have not been sorted into categories by computer, but by my own obsessive, contradictory brain. Of course, many of the quotations could fit in other categories and new categories could be created. That's your job. Use the margins, cross-reference; add the new quotations you discover to the end of the chapters in the space we've given you, use the margins, tip in new pages with glue, tape, or staple. Make my book your book.

You will note there are relatively few quotations from nonfiction writers. That isn't my fault. Nonfiction has been the principal focus of my teaching and the principal source of my income. The fact is that nonfiction writing—which produces the great majority of all writing and which outsells fiction and poetry by far—isn't taken seriously by the literary community. There are far fewer interviews with nonfiction writers and less writing about writing published by nonfiction writers. This is an area in which more students of composition should do research; rich veins of material are there ready to be mined.

writer's secrets revealed

I have read books, talks, essays, even poems by writers on writing; I have read writers' interviews, profiles, journals, letters, biographies, and autobiographies; I have worked with publishing writers and talked with them about our craft; I have taught writing to beginners and professionals and have studied my own experience in writing fiction, poetry, and a broad spectrum of nonfiction—and during this time I have discovered a set of attitudes that is remarkably similar in writers of different times, backgrounds, experience, and genre.

WHAT WRITERS SAY THAT SURPRISES

The testimony of writers often contradicts the beliefs of nonwriters and that, unfortunately, includes many teachers of writing from kindergarten through graduate school. Some of the most significant—and consistent—surprises documented in this book are:

- We surprise ourselves by what we write. Writing is thinking, not thought recorded.
- We discover how much we know rather than how little we know by writing.
- The text will teach us how it should be written if we learn how to listen to the evolving draft.
- Our voice on the page reveals what we think and how we feel.

the importance of writers' testimony

Many people have the romantic notion, encouraged by those writers who feel comfortable in the magician's robes, that writing is an instinctive matter of talent, an art, not a craft, and therefore cannot be explained.

But writing is not an unintelligent act. Writing is a craft before it is an art, and writers can and do discuss their craft in terms we can understand. There are good reasons teachers and students of writing should hear what writers say about their craft.

THE COMPANY OF WRITERS

Most writing is not collaborative. We write alone to an individual reader who hears our words alone. Those of us who live our lives as writers accept and, if we are honest, secretly delight in solitude, those hours of the day when we are alone with our developing texts.

But after the day's hours—or pages—are done, we need the fellowship of other writers. It helps to share the problems, attitudes, skills, successes we have experienced alone at our desks. We need to tell each other what it is like and share the companionship of our guild.

I will never become an Anne Tyler, Toni Morrison, William Faulkner, Gustave Flaubert, but I am comforted by what they say to me as we leave the writing desk together. My collection of quotes allows me to learn from fellow writers, to laugh and mourn with them, to know that others have experienced what I have often thought was eccentric or inappropriate.

INVITING WRITERS TO CLASS

I bring writers into my classroom through their written testimony. As writers of today and yesterday—female and male, young and old, poets and novelists and playwrights and nonfiction writers—talk about their feelings and their problems while writing, my students discover that their natural responses to writing are often the same as experienced writers.

This is vital. Students facing a writing problem will often find they have to solve it by starting over and will feel they have failed. When they read the testimony of experienced writers, however, they discover that they too act like writers and this increases their confidence in designing their own solutions to their own writing problems. School often teaches unnatural, non-writerly attitudes toward writing—know what you want to say before you say it—and students need to see that their own instincts are the instincts of publishing writers.

Students also need to see that writers are not looking back at a finished text but are in the act of confronting the blank page—or looking at the world before there is a page; trying to get started; trying to keep a text on track or following it off track; working to make a text clear to themselves and to a reader. Writer's counsel isn't distant, detached from the act of making; it is immediate, speaking to the writer in the middle of making, a master sharing the tricks of craft with an apprentice at a common workbench.

THE OPPORTUNITY FOR RESEARCH

The serious student of writing and the teacher of writing should know that the extensive testimony of writers has largely been ignored by composition researchers. What writers know about their craft has been dismissed, for example, as the "lore of the practitioner." Dr. Barbara Tomlinson of the University of California, San Diego, is the only researcher I know who has exploited this valuable resource.

Researchers usually dismiss what writers say about writing because they believe that writers do not know, intellectually, what they do. But writing is an intellectual act and writers who are able to repeat acts of effective writing demonstrably know what they are doing. And they are articulate in sharing it.

Researchers point out that writers are subjective. And they are, of course. Scholars of the writing process also point out that publishing writers do not write under the kind of research conditions inexperienced writers can be placed under in the classroom and laboratory. I would point out that often these conditions and the assignments are inappropriate if you know what writers do and how they do it.

Writers, of course, do not know everything about the complex act of making meaning through written language, but neither do researchers from any of the many schools of research. To understand how writing is made so that we can teach it more effectively we need all forms of research and the testimony of those who produce the texts we read and respect.

A NOTE ON MY INTRODUCTIONS

I do not feel the equal of the writers I quote in this book. But I hope my comments may provide a context and a bridge between the readers who need and want to study with the expert practitioners of our craft.

I also feel shy about sharing my poetry. I am not a poet—although I would like to be—but poetry is the shortest form of writing. It allows me to demonstrate matters of craft in small compass. I do not feel, however, when I am working in any form that I am facing radically different questions of craft. The problems and solutions of writing with clarity and grace cross all genre boundaries.

how to discover writers' secrets

Writers' secrets are *not* secret. There is an enormous quantity of writer testimony available. Writers have written about their craft in books about writing, in essays, in journals and notebooks, in their autobiographies, in letters, in commentary on their work and the work of other writers. They have been interviewed on radio and TV, for journals and magazines, newspapers and books. No week goes by without my reading or hearing several writers discuss their craft. The selective bibliography at the end of this book is a brief introduction to this reservoir of information about how writing is made.

how to read writers on writing

With respect, amusement, and skepticism. They will contradict one another—as they should—for each writer brings an individual history to the writing task. There is no single theology here.

What you will find is writers trying to understand what they are doing and trying to share that understanding. Their opinions may change with experience and with the writing task. It is your challenge to read these quotations in the light of your own experience writing, learning writing, teaching writing, observing writing, reading writing. You will read these bits of testimony in different ways at different times, make new connections, catch sight of new insights, keep returning to them with delight and doubt, ready to argue and to learn.

using *shoptalk* to help you learn to write

Browse through the book, reading what catches your eye. It may be something that is similar to the way you have felt when you were stuck or when the writing went well; it may be an attitude or a piece of advice that surprises you; it may be something you want to argue with, or underline. Interact with the book. Talk back, add quotes of your own, connect it with hobbies or interests of your own—playing basketball, playing the fiddle, taking photographs. Make it your own.

Look through the contents and dip into the chapters that match your concerns; perhaps you worry you are waiting too long to write, have difficulty finding a subject, feel revision is impossible. Read through those quotations, respond to them.

Turn to the Author Index and look up writers whose work you know to see what they said about the making of those books. Let them take you into their workrooms. And when you find an author whose comments on writing interest you, look up his or her books and read them.

If you are teaching literature, you may find it valuable to share what the authors you are studying say about their craft. It may provide your students with new insight and connect their own writing with their reading.

Add to the collection yourself. When you read a story in a newspaper or magazine, hear an interview on the radio or TV that provides an insight into the creative process, add it to the book. *Shoptalk* is meant to be the beginning point for your own commonplace book on writing.

1

why write

As you read through these quotations you will be impressed by the personal intensity of the writers. They are hanging on by their thumbs. They need to write. Their primary drive is not fame or fortune—although they will accept a generous serving of each—but a desperate need to understand themselves and their world. By writing they define themselves and make meaning of their experience.

Too often we defend writing as a skill, saying writing should be taught so that students can fill out a job application or write a letter asking someone to buy a cemetery lot. Writing is a skill on that level, but it is also a craft and an art; it satisfies an essential need of the human animal.

I share this need. I have been able to leave all the other jobs I have held without regret despite the deep commitment I have made to them, but I have not been able to abandon writing. I am happiest when I sit alone at my desk talking to myself on the page. Writing is my way of celebrating life and my way of escaping despair. When I am having a grumpy day, it is usually because I haven't written. I can turn the day around by spending at least a few minutes lost in an evolving draft.

This desperate personal need to write is not just felt by the writer. For more than twenty-five years, I have been conducting workshops with students and teachers, professional journalists and corporate executives. We begin by writing—writing anything that comes on the paper—and then we share what we have written.

I never cease to be surprised at what happens. Even the most private people, those who erect walls between themselves and their associates and neighbors, even their families, start to write of the most personal things: death, loss, disease, pain, driving right to the center of human experience. They write out of need as writers compose out of need.

In school and at work writing is seen as an act of testing, the way ignorance is exposed. But writing is a way of knowing, and the knowing, the understanding, is healing. We can all learn from the needs of writers—the act of writing is a constructive, helpful, and, for most of us, a necessary process.

Place yourself before a blank piece of paper or a blank computer screen. Do not intend. Wait. Or play around with some words or lines in your daybook or journal, perhaps in a draft. See what happens. Allow words to come; allow language to rearrange itself on the page. Perhaps nothing will happen. Don't worry. Try again another day.

You may feel scared. Language may hold a mirror in which you fear to look; language may, like a dream, take you where you do not want to go. It may not. It may bring you peace, understanding, comfort, insight. Your words may be happy, sad, angry, funny; you may attack, construct, tear apart, connect; you may celebrate, explore, confirm, save. You do not know what you will discover. No writer does. Fear is part of the game.

But this is a private game. You are writing to yourself. No one need see this draft; you take this adventure into the page alone. It takes courage, but in half a century of my own travels into myself and a quarter century as guide to students of all ages who make this trip, I have seen none who have not found the trip worthwhile.

Most have been willing to share their writing and have found that experience valuable; a few have made writing and sharing their life work. But sharing and publication are not important here. Writers write because of need. Share the adventure of writing with them:

- Go into yourself. Choose a place where you are comfortable. Shut the door, turn off the phone. Sit in a familiar chair at a comfortable desk or table. Go outside, sit on a bench or a rock at a beach; take a drive and sit in the car at a park, or at the edge of a parking lot, or pull off the road; take a table in a coffee shop where no one knows you; sit at a table in the library.
- Use your favorite pen or pencil, take up a pad of paper or notebook that feels good, sit before the typewriter or word processor, have the tools ready and . . .
- Wait. Enjoy the quiet. Do not fear the emptiness, welcome it, let the words come at their own time in their own order.
- Put them down. Do not judge, correct, allow shame, banish the idea of error, just record the flow.
- Read what you have written and circle what surprised you. You have shared the central experience of the writer, felt the force that compels the writer to write.

The chapters ahead will explain some of the steps in the activity I've just described. These chapters are not watertight compartments. The ideas flow back and forth between them, making new connections as all writing should.

What I've suggested for you is what I practice myself. For example, I've just been fiddling around with a poem—or some lines that might become a poem—for several weeks. On March 29, the birthday of our daughter, Lee, who died when she was twenty, I was in a meeting room at the *Boston Globe*, where I serve as writing coach. I was not consciously remembering it was Lee's birthday, but it is my habit to make use of free moments by seeing if writing comes. I enter into myself as I suggested you try. I was early, alone, and I started playing with a pen and notebook. A few lines and Lee arrived on my page. I did not welcome her visit. She brings too much pain and I had a meeting to run. But she insisted:

> Lee is 32 today, she did not stay 20
> but smiles from the shadows of every room.

This was written out of need, raw psychological need. I still cannot believe we have lost her. The act of writing does not reverse her death more than eleven years ago. It does not explain why she contracted Reye's syndrome, why she was one of the minority to die. But I must pursue the poem. I have no choice. A few days later it is finished, for the moment (*Poetry*, March 1990).

At 64, Talking without Words

The present comes clear when rubbed
with memory. I relive a childhood
of texture: oatmeal, the afternoon rug,
spears of lawn, winter finger tracing
frost on window glass, August nose
squenched against window screen. My history
of smell: bicycle oil, leather catcher's
mitt, the sweet sickening perfume of soldiers
long dead, ink fresh on the first edition.
Now I am most alone with others, companioned
by silence and the long road at my back,
mirrored by daughters. I mount the evening
stairs with mother's heavy, wearied
step, sigh my father's long complaint.
My beard grows to the sepia photograph
of a grandfather I never knew. I forget
if I turned at the bridge, but arrive
where I intended. My wife and I talk
without the bother of words. We know Lee
is 32 today. She did not stay twenty
but stands at each room's doorway. I place
my hand on the telephone. It rings.

I have written for many reasons: to feed my family and myself, to get ahead, to exercise power, to call attention to myself, to be published, to understand, to entertain, to make something that is my own, to find out what I have to say, and, above all, from need. And, as you will discover if you share the writer's world, there is often comfort and even a strange celebration in such writing as in this poem. I can't explain it, but I must do it.

Edward Albee
I write to find out what I'm thinking about.

Anita Brookner
I started writing because of a terrible feeling of powerlessness.

Rosellen Brown
Writing is the creation of fantasies that please you, that fill your own needs.

Hortense Calisher
The novel is rescued life.

John Cheever
It seems to me that writing is a marvelous way of making sense of one's life, both for the writer and for the reader.

John Ciardi
The artist writes compulsively, as a way of knowing himself. . . . He writes for those glimpses of order that form can make momentarily visible.

Joseph Conrad
I don't like work—no man does—but I like what is in the work—the chance to find yourself.

Joan Didion
Had I been blessed with even limited access to my own mind there would have been no reason to write. I write entirely to find out what I'm thinking, what I'm looking at, what I see and what it means. What I want and what I fear.

John Dos Passos
Curiosity urges you on—the driving force.

T. S. Eliot
What stimulates me to write a poem is that I have got something inside me that I want to get rid of—it is almost a kind of defecation.

Louise Erdrich
Part of becoming a writer is the desire to have everything mean something.

William Faulkner
The aim of the artist is to arrest motion, which is life. A hundred years later, a stranger looks at it, and it moves again.

Robert Frost
You know, I've often said that every poem solves something for me in life. I go so far as to say that every poem is a momentary stay against the confusion of the world.

William Gibson
Writing for me was always an inside thing. It's always been the way in which I maintain my sanity.

Herbert Gold
I write to master my experience.

Graham Greene
Writing is a form of therapy; sometimes I wonder how all those who do not write, compose or paint can manage to escape the madness, the melancholia, the panic fear which is inherent in the human situation.

John Hawkes
Fiction is an act of revenge.

Ernest Hemingway
From things that have happened and from things as they exist and from things that you know and all those you cannot know, you make something through your invention that is not a representation but a whole new thing truer than anything true and alive, and you make it alive, and if you make it well enough, you give it immortality. That is why you write and for no other reason that you know of.

Cecelia Holland
One of the reasons a writer writes, I think, is that his stories reveal so much he never thought he knew.

Jacqueline Jackson
I'm sure a beautiful empty notebook was the reason I wrote my first book. It was begging for filling.

Samuel Johnson
I write; therefore, I am.

James Jones
I do think that the quality which makes a man want to write and be read is essentially a desire for self-exposure and is masochistic. Like one of those guys who has a complusion to take his thing out and show it on the street.

Franz Kafka
A book should serve as the axe for the frozen sea within us.

Alfred Kazin
In a very real sense, the writer writes in order to teach himself, to understand himself, to satisfy himself; the publishing of his ideas, though it brings gratifications, is a curious anticlimax.

Garrison Keillor
Despite all the changes and upsets and the general disjointedness of so much of the rest of my life, writing is the one seam that runs straight through—one of the few. That's why I consider myself a writer. It is an act I perform every day. It is an act by which I hope to come to some peace with myself and my past, as every writer does, I think.

David Leavitt
I find that process has started to become essential to me in my life, just as it is to take walks, to exercise, to eat, to ride a bicycle. It's part of maintaining myself in the world, of keeping myself healthy.

Doris Lessing
I write because I've always written, can't stop, I'm a writing animal. The way a silk-worm is a silk-producing animal.

C. Day Lewis
We do not write in order to be understood, we write in order to understand.

Anne Morrow Lindbergh
An experience isn't finished until it's written.

Alison Lurie

I found that it was boring *not* to write. It made the world emptier and thinner for me.

Ross MacDonald

I don't think people become writers, for the most part, unless they have experienced a peculiar distancing, which generally occurs in childhood or youth and makes the direct satisfactions of living unsatisfactory, so that one has to seek one's basic satisfactions indirectly through what we can loosely call art. What makes the verbal artist is some kind of shock or crippling or injury which puts the world at one removed from him, so that he writes about it to take possession of it. . . . We start out thinking we're writing about other people and end up realizing we're writing about ourselves.

Somerset Maugham

We do not write because we want to; we write because we must.

William Maxwell

And while he is asleep he may dream—he may dream that he had a dream, in which the whole meaning of what he is trying to say is brilliantly revealed to him. Just so the dog asleep on the hearth—rug dreams; you can see, by the faint jerking movement of his four legs, that he is after a rabbit. The writer's rabbit is the truth—about life, about human character, about himself and therefore by extension, it is to be hoped, about other people.

He is convinced that all this is knowable, can be described, can be recorded, by a person sufficiently dedicated to describing and recording; can be caught in a net of narration.

Heather McHugh

I began to write because I was too shy to talk, and too lonely not to send messages.

H. L. Mencken

His overpowering impulse is to gyrate before his fellow man, flapping his wings and emitting defiant yells. This being forbidden by the police of all civilized countries, he takes it out by putting his yells on paper. Such is the thing called self-expression.

Czeslaw Milosz

To find my home in one sentence, concise, as if hammered in metal. Not to enchant anybody. Not to earn a lasting name in posterity. An unnamed need for order, for rhythm, for form, which three words are opposed to chaos and nothingness.

Alberto Moravia
I write in order to know why I write.

Toni Morrison
Writing was the only work I did that was for myself and by myself. In the process, one exercises sovereignty in a special way. All sensibilities are engaged, sometimes simultaneously, sometimes sequentially. While I'm writing, all of my experience is vital and useful and possibly important.

V. S. Naipaul
To write was to learn. Beginning a book, I always felt I was in possession of all the facts about myself; at the end I was always surprised.

Anais Nin
We write to taste life twice, in the moment, and in retrospection.

Joyce Carol Oates
All art is autobiographical. It is the record of an artist's psychic experience, his attempt to explain something to himself: and in the process of explaining it to himself, he explains it to others.

Flannery O'Connor
I write because I don't know what I think until I read what I say.

Eugene O'Neill
Writing is my vacation from living.

George Orwell
All writers are vain, selfish, and lazy, and at the very bottom of their motives there lies a mystery. Writing a book is a horrible, exhausting struggle, like a long bout of some painful illness. One would never undertake such a thing if one were not driven on by some demon whom one can never resist or understand. For all one knows that demon is simply the same instinct that makes a baby squall for attention.

V. S. Pritchett
I write to clear my own mind, to find out what I think and feel.

Jean Rhys
I wrote it because it relieved me.

Maurice Sendak
You write or paint because you have to. THERE IS NO CHOICE.

Mary Lee Settle

I did not want to write it. But in order to find out what I wanted to know, I had to.

Susan Sontag

The subject becomes unbearably present to me, so that I almost have to write it to get it out of my head.

Wallace Stegner

We do not write what we know; we write what we want to find out.

Barbara Tuchman

I have always been in a condition in which I cannot *not* write.

Anne Tyler

For me, writing something down was the only road out. . . . I hated childhood, and spent it sitting behind a book waiting for adulthood to arrive. When I ran out of books I made up my own. At night, when I couldn't sleep, I made up stories in the dark.

Diane Wakoski

I was born into a desert of silence. I was surrounded by silent people when I was young. I was silent and still, as a child. And I only learned to talk in school, as a formal raise-your-hand, teacher-calls-on-you, recite-the-answer gesture. So the poem, as a formal gesture, allows me to raise my hand, to be called on and to speak.

Robert Penn Warren

. . .The urge to write poetry is like having an itch. When the itch becomes annoying enough, you scratch it.

E. B. White

I haven't told why I wrote the book *[Charlotte's Web]*, but I haven't told why I sneeze either. A book is a sneeze.

Elie Wiesel

Writing is a duty for me as a survivor. I entered literature through silence; I seek the role of witness, and I am dutybound to justify each moment of my life as a survivor.

Joy Williams

One writes to find words' meaning.

other quotations that help me write:

_____

other quotations that help me write:

other quotations that help me write:
_____

2

the writer's world

I remember childhood as a time of almost desperate awareness. I was an only child in a house of huge adults: grandmother, mother, father, Uncle Will. I remember each of our homes when I was small by the places I hid listening, watching, trying to understand.

The quotations in this chapter reveal the writer at work collecting the raw material from which writing will be made. Art begins in awareness. Writers see implication in what others pass by, noticing the extraordinary in the ordinary, using image and word to articulate feelings and thoughts. Writers draw from the well of awareness that never seems to run dry.

In a moment I can return to the head of the stairs where I sat when I was eight years old to overhear the living room conversations of visiting grown-ups; my ear can still feel the cold metal of the cast-iron heating grate that allowed heat—and secrets—to float from the kitchen to the bedroom above; I can smell the dank black earth under the porch and hear the rocking, rocking of the chairs above where they talked of what could be said when the child was not around.

As I mentioned in the poem in the last chapter, we each have a history of texture and a history of smell. I could have added taste. All our senses record the world, and in the act of writing we recover what we cannot remember. I do not have a good memory in the TV game-show sense, but when I am writing, I see again, hear again, call on what was recorded unaware. It is there waiting to be enlisted in the search for meaning.

And that compulsive need to observe, capture, and examine the world has been a blessing. Even in school, even in the army, even in faculty meetings, it has kept me from boredom. I have the writer's gift of being able to observe revealing details—what is not said, as well as what is said, the gesture made and not made, the pause, the pale square on the wallpaper where a picture once hung.

Try a list. Watch children as Tom Newkirk has in *More Than Stories* (Heinemann, 1989), and you will discover the intellectual power of the list. Allow your mind to pursue one subject but don't worry if your mind hops around. Much good writing comes from associating, a powerful type of thinking unfortunately not often taught or tolerated in school.

If you think back to a significant incident in your life, you will discover you remember more than you observed. Your brain recorded it and you can draw on it years, even decades, later. Don't worry if you have a poor memory. I do. But writing draws out of memory what can't be recalled any other way. And remember to record with all your senses. A list, from memory, will reveal what is there.

Another way to make a list is to sit and observe, recording specifics you see, hear, smell, taste, touch. As you notice more, what you notice increases. Awareness leads to increased awareness. This is one of the great joys of writing.

After you have made a memory or an observation list, read it over. Circle what surprised you; draw lines connecting details that reveal the same thing. You may have the beginning of a piece of writing. And when you write from the list, you will discover new material not on the list that fits what you are discovering to say.

Specifics combine with details from past and present, details read and heard and dreamt and imagined, so that meaning is revealed in the writer's mind and on the writer's page. The specifics grow into phrases, sentences, stories, poems, essays.

In writing the following poem, I became "aware" of the world before I consciously remembered it and moved forward to a moment I haven't yet experienced. I don't know where that china cabinet is now—my mother was a great get-ridder of things. But by living in the poem I realized how much I had used the reflections in that glass door to allow me to observe without the spied upon being aware of the spy in their midst.

Reunion

I remember the moment when I found my face
looking out the glass door of the china cabinet.
My head so large, my tadpole body squirming
along the rug behind. So this was me.

Behind me I watch the shadowed legs of grown-ups.
I smell the mystery of skirts. The china cabinet
records my first quavering stand alone, how I take
stairs two at a time, look at my watch, leave home.

Returning, I bring the only beard to the family dinner
but my rebellious whiskers hang on grandfather's portrait.

I am mirrored by daughters, remember when I needed three
phone books to sit on these chairs and reach turkey.

I grow quiet over pie and they ask how I feel.
I am that age. I smile and tell a story, they smile
as if they had heard it all before. They had. I turn
to watch my face fading in the china cabinet door.

Awareness makes writing possible—and, as mentioned, writing increases awareness. While we are writing we recognize the significance of what we remember and what we did not know we remembered, enabling us to "remember" what we have not yet experienced. When we become masters of awareness we write with concrete information with which we shape meaning. Language allows us to fit information into unexpected patterns, seeing our world this way and that, from the outside in and inside out, standing far away and close up until we can create a text in which others can glimpse our individual vision of our shared world.

John Ashbery
I can't tell you why a certain overheard remark seems significant and another one doesn't except that when I'm in a state of attentiveness, waiting to write a poem, I can tell intuitively what's going to help me to write and what isn't. All I need is the time and a not too depressed state of mind to be able to start concentrating attentively in order to pick up whatever is in the air.

James Baldwin
The importance of a writer . . . is that he is here to describe things which other people are too busy to describe.

John Barth
The scene inside your house, inside your head, is more important than the scene outside.

Saul Bellow
I begin to get preconscious intimations of what the work is going to be like, even before I awaken. I see faces and scenes, floors, walls, landscapes. I hear lines of dialogue.

Judy Blume

I don't *tell* the story to myself—I *see* it. I see scenes, and I write down what I see. I hear the characters talking to each other.

Catherine Drinker Bowen

Writing is a kind of double living. The writer experiences everything twice. Once in reality and once in that mirror which waits always before or behind him.

Elizabeth Bowen

The writer . . . sees what he did not expect to see. . . . Inattentive learner in the schoolroom of life, he keeps some faculty free to hear and wonder. His is the roving eye. By that roving eye is his subject found. The glance, at first only vaguely caught, goes on to concentrate, deepen; becomes the vision.

Anita Brookner

. . . for the writer there is no oblivion. Only endless memory.

Morley Callaghan

There is only one trait that marks the writer. He is always watching.

Albert Camus

An intellectual is someone whose mind watches itself.

Willa Cather

Most of the basic material a writer works with is acquired before the age of fifteen.

Paul Cézanne

I could keep myself busy for months without moving from one spot, just by leaning now to the right, now to the left.

Anton Chekhov

An artist observes, selects, guesses, and combines.

Joseph Conrad

My task . . . is, by the power of the written word, to make you hear, to make you feel—it is, before all, to make you see.

Alfred Coppel

I visualize, then write about what I see.

James Dickey

That could almost be cited as the definition of a poet: Someone who notices and is enormously taken by things that somebody else would walk by.

E. L. Doctorow

A novelist is a person who lives in other people's skins.

William Faulkner

Memory believes before knowing remembers.

Gustave Flaubert

. . . it is a delicious thing to write, to be no longer yourself but to move in an entire universe of your own creating. Today, for instance, as man and woman, both lover and mistress, I rode in a forest on an autumn afternoon under the yellow leaves, and I was also the horses, the leaves, the wind, the words my people uttered, even the red sun that made them almost close their love-drowned eyes.

C. S. Forester

Sitting at a writing table writing words on paper, what is it that forms these words? What is going on in my mind as I write them? I have no doubt that in my case it is a matter of a series of visualizations. Not two-dimensional, as if I were looking at a television screen; three-dimensional perhaps, as if I were a thin, thin, invisible ghost walking about on a stage while a play is in actual performance.

John Fowles

The novel I am writing at the moment [provisionally entitled *The French Lieutenant's Woman*] . . . started four or five months ago as a visual image. A woman stands at the end of a deserted quay and stares out to sea. That was all.

Pamela Frankau

There must come a time when . . . all your mirrors turn into windows.

Ellen Glasgow

I suppose I am a born novelist, for the things I imagine are more vital and vivid to me than the things I remember.

Graham Greene

When I construct a scene, I don't describe the hundredth part of what I see; I see the characters scratching their noses, walking about, tilting back in their chairs—even after I've finished writing—so much so that after a while I feel a weariness which does not derive all that much from my effort of imagination but is more like a visual fatigue: My eyes are tired from watching my characters.

Nancy Hale

The writer is a person who goes around in a state of skinlessness.

Hokusai

If you want to draw a bird, you must become a bird.

Henrik Ibsen

Before I write down one word, I have to have the character in mind through and through. I must penetrate into the last wrinkle of his soul. I always proceed from the individual; the stage setting, the dramatic ensemble, all of that comes naturally and does not cause me to worry, as soon as I am certain of the individual in every aspect of his humanity. But I have to have his exterior in mind also, down to the last button, how he stands and walks, how he conducts himself, what his voice sounds like. Then I do not let him go until his fate is fulfilled.

Eugene Ionesco

I am always surprised. I go through life perpetually astonished at everything that happens around me.

John Irving

A fiction writer's memory is an especially imperfect provider of detail; we can always imagine a better detail than the one we can remember. The correct detail is rarely, exactly, what happened; the most truthful detail is what *could* have happened, or what *should* have.

Christopher Isherwood

I am a camera with its shutter open, quite passive, recording not thinking. Recording the man shaving at the window opposite and the woman in the kimono washing her hair. Some day, all this will have to be developed, carefully fixed, printed.

Henry James

Try to be one of the people on whom nothing is lost.

John Keats

I looked out the window and saw a sparrow and I became the sparrow. I saw a piece of straw and I became the straw.

Milan Kundera

But isn't it true that an author can write only about himself?

Staring impotently across a courtyard, at a loss for what to do; hearing the pertinacious rumbling of one's own stomach during a moment of love; betraying, yet lacking the will to abandon the glamorous path of betrayal; raising one's fist with the crowds in the Grand March; displaying one's wit before hidden microphones—I have known all these situations, I have experienced them myself, yet none of them has given rise to the person my curriculum vitae and I represent. The characters in my novels are my own unrealized possibilities. . . . Each one has crossed a border I myself have circumvented . . . beyond that border begins the secret the novel asks about. . . .

John Le Carré

. . . like a spy, the writer moves among his fellow-men with nostalgia, envy and revulsion; it is this tenuous, painful unease which tautens his perception and forces him to communicate.

Bernard Malamud

You learn from the imaginative what the real world is.

Katherine Mansfield

I've *been* this man, *been* this woman. I've stood for hours on the Auckland Wharf. I've been out in the stream waiting to be berthed—I've been a seagull hovering at the stern and a hotel porter whistling through his teeth.

Somerset Maugham

The author does not only write when he's at his desk, he writes all day long, when he is thinking, when he is reading, when he is experiencing; everything he sees and feels is significant to his purpose and, consciously or unconsciously, he is forever storing and making over his impressions.

Guy de Maupassant

For him no simple feeling exists. All that he sees, his joys, his pleasures, his suffering, his despair, all instantaneously become objects of observation. . . . He has not a spark of enthusiasm, not a cry, not a kiss that is spontaneous, not one instantaneous action done merely because it must be done, unconsciously, without understanding, without writing it down afterwards. He says to himself as he leaves the cemetery where he has left the being he loved most in the world; it is curious what I felt . . .

Carson McCullers

I become the characters I write about. I am so immersed in them that their motives are my own. When I write about a thief, I become one;

when I write about Captain Penderton, I become a homosexual man; when I write about a deaf mute, I become dumb during the time of the story. I become the characters I write about and I bless the Latin poet Terence who said, "Nothing human is alien to me."

Vladimir Nabokov

I don't think in any language. I think in images. I don't believe that people think in languages.

Joyce Carol Oates

. . . before I begin to write I "see" a story completely, often down to the very length and rhythm of paragraphs and sentences. I visualize the characters completely; I have heard their dialogue, I know how they speak, what they want, who they are, nearly everything about them that touches upon this central crisis in their lives. Then, when I write the story or the scene, I am only remembering, re-constructing an event that has already taken place. I don't make it up as I write. Never. I spend a great deal of time simply walking around, sitting, day-dreaming, going through the motions of an ordinary life with—I suspect—an abstracted, dreamy, rather blank expression on my face.

Edna O'Brien

I sometimes think that writers are the great pretenders of all times. They feel everything both more and less. Without question, they are split people, experiencing and observing at one and the same time.

Reynolds Price

The stories have arrived, the novels have arrived then as sudden visual pictures.

Theodore Roethke

Nothing seen, nothing said.

Lillian Ross

One of the conspicuous things about Aubrey, Defoe, Turgenev, and Mayhew is that they were all enraptured by facts. They tried to set down what could be seen and heard and touched, what could be tested and confirmed by others: what was true. They wrote about particulars; they didn't generalize. They didn't analyze; they tried to understand but not overinterpret. They did not indulge in flourishes; they did not feel a need to show off. All of them wrote at times in the first person, but none of them called attention to himself. Their interest was in *what-they-were-writing-about*. All were people who had genuine curiosity about other people and about how things worked. All had highly developed powers of observation.

Philip Roth
. . . while you're in the midst of a story, so many things in your daily life seem to apply to it—you see something on the bus and think how you can use it. The story's like a magnet and without it, you'd never notice all these things.

William Sansom
A writer lives, at best, in a state of astonishment. Beneath any feeling he has of the good or evil of the world lies a deeper one of wonder at it all. To transmit that feeling, he writes.

P. B. Shelley
[The poet] is the tireless collector of the looks and sounds and shapes and feel of things.

Georges Simenon
I'm a bit like a sponge. When I'm not writing I absorb life like water. When I write I squeeze the sponge a little—and out it comes, not water but ink.

Neil Simon
I always picture myself as that person at a cocktail party standing in the corner and watching.

Wallace Stevens
The tongue is an eye.

William Styron
I woke up one spring morning after having been in this funk over a book I was involved in—namely a book about the Marine Corps that I'd been writing for several years and which was proceeding slowly without much inspiration. I sensed I had dreamed a vision of a girl named Sophie whom I remembered from Brooklyn in the postwar years. She was a very vivid image in my mind and in my dream. When I woke up I lay there for quite a long time with a sense that (and I don't mean to sound fancy or imply that this was a psychic experience because it wasn't), . . . I had almost been given a mandate to write this book. I saw the whole thing plain: the idea of combining the Sophie story with the story I had heard of another victim of the camps who had to make a choice between her children—all this seen through the eyes of a young man. It was almost as if the story was outlined . . . I knew roughly what I was going to do with the book the day I set the first words of it down, which was the day I woke up with that dream.

William Trevor

I think there's something *in* writers of fiction that makes them notice things and store them away all the time. You *notice* the cherry red. Writers of fiction are collectors of useless information. They are the opposite of good, solid, wise citizens who collect good information and put it to good use. Fiction writers remember tiny little details, some of them almost malicious, but very telling. It's a way of endlessly remembering. A face comes back after years and years and years, as though you've taken a photograph. It's as though you have, for the moment, thought: "I know that person very well." You could argue that you have some extraordinary insight, but actually it's just a very hard-working imagination. It's almost like a stress in you that goes on, nibbling and nibbling, gnawing away at you, in a *very* inquisitive way, wanting to know. And of course while all that's happening you're stroking in the colors, putting a line here and a line there, creating something which moves further and further away from the original. The truth emerges, the person who is created is a different person altogether—a person in their own right.

Anne Tyler

I guess I work from a combination of curiosity and distance. It seems to me often that I'm sort of looking from a window at something at a great distance and wondering what it is. But I'm not willing to actually go into it. I would rather sit behind the windowsill and write about it. So all my curiosity has to be answered within myself instead of by crossing the street and asking what's going on.

John Updike

All I have to go on is something I caught a glimpse of out of the corner of my eye.

Paul Valéry

To observe amounts for the most part to imagining what one expects to see.

Edward Lewis Wallant

We speak of art and we speak of illumination; in order to illuminate for others, one must obviously first be able to see for himself. Seeing is the key word, seeing with the heart, with the brain, with the eye.

Eudora Welty

Making pictures of people in all sorts of situations, I learn that every feeling waits upon its gesture; and I had to be prepared to recognize this moment when I saw it.

Walt Whitman
I do not ask the wounded person how he feels—I myself become the wounded person.

John Wideman
Distance is essential. You stand on the outside and you look in. You can't become totally involved in anything. You've got to step aside to see it so you can understand it. You pay your dues for doing that. You can cut yourself off from your feelings.

Tennessee Williams
When I write, everything is visual, as brilliantly as if it were on a lit stage. And I talk out the lines as I write.

other quotations that help me write:

other quotations that help me write:

3

out of silence, words

My students often told me they didn't have anything to say. They were silent. Empty. They felt anxiety. Panic. Terror.

"Good," I'd answer. "You are a writer. You are at the place from which writing comes. And you feel the way the writer feels at the center of silence."

Eventually they would find that I spoke the truth. And if they became writers, they discovered they had to be seekers of silence. The more skilled they were at our craft, the easier it was to write, the greater number of tricks they had in their magician's bag, the more important it was that they drove themselves back to the moment of silence from which important writing comes.

We are drawn to silence and terrified by it. Writing is our way of escape. It is the central irony of our art that we must sentence ourselves over and over again to the silence from which we will struggle to escape, unless we are willing to flip fast-food hamburgers of writing all our life.

Of course, a writer's silence may be encouraged by the proper sound. I encourage silence by listening to Mozart—or Beethoven, Dvořák, Schubert, Bach, or Goodman, Ellington, Lester Young, Teddy Wilson—but I can't have music in which English is sung. My son-in-law, who is a composer, listens to talk shows, not music, while he works.

Often I find silence watching mindless TV, a cops-and-robbers show or the Boston Red Sox, who never produce enough excitement to involve all of my brain. I may find silence in a coffee shop busy with strangers, while shopping in bookstores or stationery stores. It is an internal silence, an envelope of mental quiet, in which I can hear what writing is whispering to me.

As writers we have to find our own way back to an essential stage of ignorance when we do not know—not know what to say, not know how to say. We have to be at the beginning point of ignorance, ignorance of content and technique, the initiating point of naiveté, of innocence. We have to learn our own way of achieving this essential retroactive virginity.

I have to peel back what I have done before, forget the lessons I have learned, what I have published, even what others have published, allowing research, memory, experience, feeling and thought to pass through me as if it were the first time.

Of course I do not achieve it. Skill, experience, accomplishment weigh on me; I envy the beginning writer who has the advantage of silence, emptiness, the essential terror of not knowing. Don't flee from it, accept it, cultivate it. Right now, choose your own way—a walk in the woods, Mozart on the hi fi, a back table in a strange coffee shop, sit, wait, listen.

John Ashbery
I actually try to begin writing with my mind a tabula rasa; I don't want to know, can't know what I'm going to write.

Margaret Atwood
Poems begin somewhere off the page. You hear pieces of them, sometimes the whole poem. When you have the equipment you write them down. If you start writing down too soon you may lose the rest of the poem. . . . All you can do is wait, and make doodles in the margins.

Saul Bellow
I feel that art has something to do with the achievement of stillness in the midst of chaos. A stillness which characterizes prayer, too, and the eye of the storm. I think that art has something to do with an arrest of attention in the midst of distraction.

James Carroll
Writers have another conviction. We believe, and this is what makes us writers, that in silence the truth reveals itself.

Rachel Carson
The discipline of the writer is to learn to be still and listen to what his subject has to tell him.

Blanche D'Alpuget
There's only one that that's important and that is that there are no interruptions, that the telephone doesn't ring. I have to get very deeply inside myself and I have to get very still. If you have to stop suddenly

and you have to talk to somebody, you've got to put on this whole
new personality to meet them, and it just pulls you out of that place of
stillness.

E. L. Doctorow

One of the things I've discovered about writing is that you have to sink
way down to a level of hopelessness and desperation to find the book
that you can write.

Peter Everwine

I believe in luck. I believe in training yourself to go to a place and sit and
to try to get in touch with a voice that you listen to inside of yourself.
And maybe that's what I understand by inspiration. The notion of sitting
with yourself, of trying to come to grips with your own sense of experience, with what the world does outside of you. Maybe it is akin to the
act of meditation. Maybe that's what inspiration is, the removing stuff
that keeps you from the outside world.

William H. Gass

But what do beginners know? too much. It is what they think they
know that makes them beginners.

Nadine Gordimer

The solitude of writing is also quite frightening. It's quite close sometimes to madness, one just disappears for a day and loses touch.

Robert Hayden

. . . a poem should have silences. For me the silences of a poem are as
meaningful as its sounds. All my best poems have silences in them.
There are things in them that are not expressed, that are all the more
strongly suggested because they are not stated.

Shirley Hazzard

The attempt to touch truth through a work of imagination requires an
inner center of privacy and solitude. We all need silence—both external
and interior—in order to find out what we truly think.

Philip Levine

I don't so nearly search for my poems as they find me. I don't run away
from them. Which is what I see some people do. I mean, there's no way
the poem is going to find you if you're playing ping-pong. Or cha-cha-
chaing. Chasing girls, or whatever it is you chase. Perfecting your back
stroke. I mean, there's no way. You have to be there. In some state of
readiness and hospitality to the fucking muse, you know, who is, after

all, only a part of you. You have to let it open the door and come into your brain, into your hand, wherever it comes. And I do a lot of that. I mean I sit long hours picking my nose. I don't even pick my nose. I do nothing. I've learned that you have to do nothing. You have to be silent and see if the voice will enter you.

Henry Miller

... most writing is done away from the typewriter, away from the desk. I'd say it occurs in the quiet, silent moments. . . .

Joyce Carol Oates

If you are a writer, you locate yourself behind a wall of silence and no matter what you are doing, driving a car or walking or doing house-work, which I love, you can still be writing, because you have that space.

Octavio Paz

Many times I feel empty, without ideas—and then suddenly the first sentence appears.

Walker Percy

The only thing I can say is that it takes place—or the best of it takes place—in a sort of vacuum. On the worst of mornings. On the least likely of mornings. When you expect nothing to happen. When the page is blank. When the mind is blank. Even in a state of depression or melancholia. And then, only with good luck. I sometimes get the feeling that the slate has to be wiped completely clean, that there can be no prospects, nothing pending, nothing coming in the afternoon or the next day, that there has to be some sort of vacuum in order for something else to come out.

*

I remember something Franz Kafka wrote. He had a motto, *"Warte,"* written on the wall over his bed. *Wait.* You don't have to worry, you don't have to press, you don't have to force the muse, or whatever it is. All you have to do is wait.

*

On those days or mornings when you feel worst, when you think every-thing is hopeless, that nothing will happen—sometimes the *best* things happen.

Marge Piercy

If you can lose a novel by talking it out, you can easily destroy a poem by not paying attention. I have lost many poems that way; I must lose one a week because I can't get to a typewriter or even to a piece of

paper fast enough—sometimes can't break through to silence, to solitude, to a closed door.

Katherine Anne Porter

I prefer to get up very early in the morning and work. I don't want to
speak to anybody or see anybody. Perfect silence.

Philip Roth

The concentration of writing requires silence. For me, large blocks of
silence. It's like hearing a faint Morse code—a faint signal is being
given, and I need quiet to pick it up.

*

I think that temperamentally most writers are drawn to solitude and
seclusion. Otherwise they couldn't tolerate the job. They couldn't bear
the uneventfulness of the work.

Charles Simic

In the end, I'm always at the beginning. Silence—an endless mythical
condition. I think of explorers setting out over an unknown ocean, the
distant light they see at the horizon in a direction where there's no
known land.

August Strindberg

Ever since my youth my morning walk has been dedicated to meditation
as a preparation for the day's work. I have never allowed anyone to
accompany me, not even my wife. . . . It is for me the hour of inward
concentration, the hour of prayer, of worship.

John Updike

A few places are specially conducive to inspiration—automobiles,
church—private places. I plotted *Couples* almost entirely in church—
little shivers and urgencies I would note down on the program, and
carry down to the office Monday.

Alice Walker

✓ If you're silent for a long time, people just arrive in your mind.

Robert Penn Warren

Solitude is *blankness* that makes accidents happen.

Elie Wiesel

Before I write I must endure the silence, then the silence breaks out. In
the beginning there was silence—no words. The word itself is a breaking out. The word itself is an act of violence; it breaks the silence. We

cannot avoid the silence, we must not. What we can do is somehow change words with silence. If one of my novels is only words, without silence, I don't even reread or publish it. The unspoken is as important as the spoken: the weight of silence is necessary. To speak about silence is to reduce it, but in every book I do speak about silence. There are zones of silence, there are shades of silence. Silence has its own archaeology, its own memory, its own colors: it's dark and gray and long and short and harsh and soft. Silence is the universe itself.

Jeanette Winterson

. . . the way I work best is to be entirely alone. And during that period your characters are really the only people you can have a conversation with, because no one else is there, and the world you're creating becomes a real world, and the rest, what is supposed to be the most solid and best known, is really only shadows.

William Wordsworth

. . . a wise passiveness.

other quotations that help me write:

_____

other quotations that help me write:

other quotations that help me write:

_____

4

---

write for yourself—then others

First, be yourself. You don't have any choice. That's your curse and your opportunity: you must write yourself. And that is a significant irony in most writers' lives, certainly mine.

I think I began writing—telling myself stories, day dreaming and night dreaming, walking around in a fantasy world in which I was cop or robber, cowboy or Indian, football hero or baseball star, great lover or at least a kid who could get a date—to escape myself.

I did not like myself or my lot in life. I felt I was nothing and so I made up lives in which I had power, success, control. And I led those lives in my mind so effectively that my teachers failed to get my mind to climb back through the window and attend class and my mother would wave her hand in front of my face at supper and I would go on chomping, not seeing it until she commanded, "Donald. Pay attention. Now."

And so the escape of writing in my head became writing on paper and it was my trade, almost before I knew it, and I discovered that as I wrote I revealed myself on the page. That self from which I had been engineering my escape was there for everyone to see, including myself.

Writers talk here of finding themselves on the page. I wonder if they *wanted* to find themselves. I didn't. I wanted to go into space, track a moose in the north woods, take June Allyson to a Vermont inn for the weekend. But there I was, writing of what I saw, thought, felt, imagined in my language and my voice. I didn't write like Robert Louis Stevenson, Sir Walter Scott, Kenneth Roberts, A. E. Housman; I wrote like that weird kid from North Quincy, the gawky one with the glasses, the cowlick, and the huge hands he didn't know where to put, that skinny one standing in the corner. Alone. Watching.

I am still a bit uncomfortable writing this way, revealing myself in these chapter introductions, not being academic but autobiographical, self-centered, self-revealing. But that is all I've got. My world as I know it, my voice as I can tune it.

Even in the corporate world, the writer is egocentric, obsessed with self. That is what each writer, no matter the mode or form of writing, has to offer: the individual view and the individual voice.

It is the hardest and the best instruction: be yourself. And in being yourself, becoming most individual and most personal, you will discover that you are articulating what other individuals know but cannot say. By turning inward, you will achieve community.

And how do you do this? Well, writers do it by writing. We try—and failing, try again—to be honest on the page: to look directly at life, then find the word, the phrase, the line that describes what we see, tells us what it means, reveals what we feel. And the miracle is that if we reveal—deeply and honestly—our vision, we will discover we have given eye and voice to the vision of others.

Yet we are still our own first readers. We write to educate ourselves, to explore and explain our world, to celebrate and preserve that world, to entertain and console ourselves, to express ourselves and share our vision of our world.

I write for myself but even as I write I am aware of my private readers, those who will see my pages first. They are test readers and they change according to what I am writing. In this case, a small community of writers who read the first draft: my wife and daughters, who are always my first readers; Chip Scanlan, to whom the book is dedicated; Ann Vibert, with whom it has been discussed; my editors Bob Boynton, Philippa Stratton, and especially Toby Gordon.

I have developed—and cultivated—my own community of writers whom I enlist as my editors to help me with my writing. Each teaches me in his or her own way. It is their faces I see while writing. I know, at the moment of writing, that Chip will appreciate this phrase, Mekeel will nod at this line, Don will get the joke.

My readers will change a bit from genre to genre, the way you may not invite someone for dinner when you are going to serve sauerkraut, but most of them are at my writing desk. Minnie Mae, who may read what I have written on the screen, my daughters Anne and Hannah, Tom and Tom, Mary Ellen, Nancie, Brock, Penny, Linda, Driek, Bill, Tilly and John.

These readers who live in D.C. and N.Y.C., Idaho and Maine, Utah and Virginia, Wyoming and Massachusetts, Ohio and New Hampshire do not all know one another but they have several qualities in common:

• They like me and like how I write. [I wrote that line, then debated a long time about leaving it in, but feel I must. I discovered its importance in its writing. Their responses are supportive and sympathetic for what I am trying to do, although they may not agree with how I have done it.]

- They know writing, understand the risks of our craft, and expose themselves in their work.
- They are perceptive readers, secure enough to give support, skilled enough to give criticism, and able to read my drafts *with my intentions in mind.* That last quality is exceedingly rare. They do not try to make me write the texts they want to write in the way they would write them; they want me to write not for them but for me.
- I want to write after they have talked to me about my writing. Their response may be praise or criticism or a combination of both, but they inspire me to write. After a lunch or phone call or letter, I immediately start writing in my head or on the word processor.

Consider my guidelines and start your own writing community. It doesn't need to be large, one good reader, or two or three, is fine. They don't have to live next door. They do, however, each in his or her own way, have to help you write not for them but for yourself.

And a word about editors. They too can be destructive: forcing their intentions on your writing, responding in a way inappropriate to the stage you are at in the writing, insisting on putting their mark—like a male dog on a walk—on each page. If you want to become published you will have to find your own survival techniques to work with them.

But we need editors. When you find a good one, cultivate them. I asked for Toby Gordon on this book since she had helped on the last one and my previous editor is on maternity leave. I let Toby—and her editor—know I thought she was good. I responded warmly and candidly to her reading and have invited her to help me. I need it. I treat her the way I want to be treated when I serve as editor. We need each other, but if I am to produce work worth editing, I first have to write for myself.

Edward Albee
   I write for me. For the audience of me. If other people come along for the ride then it's great.

Robert Anderson
   Every play I have written is me. I am naked when I finish.

Jane Austen
   [Writing an answer to Prince Regent's librarian who asked her to write an historical romance:]

No, I must keep to my own style, and go on in my own way; and though I may never succeed *again* in that, I am convinced that I should totally fail in any other.

Toni Cade Bambara
First and foremost I write for myself. Writing has been for a long time my major tool for self-instruction and self-development. I try to stay honest through pencil and paper.

John Barth
There are writers whose gift is to make terribly complicated things simple. But I know my gift is the reverse: to take relatively simple things and complicate them to the point of madness. But there you are: one learns who one is, and it is at one's peril that one attempts to become someone else.

Saul Bellow
I think a writer is on track when the door of his native and deeper intuitions is open. You write a sentence that doesn't come from that source and you can't build around it—it makes the page seem somehow false.

Ingrid Bengis
By the time I sat down at the typewriter, I was writing a book quite unlike the one I had at first planned to write, because I was quite unlike the person who had first considered writing it.

Edmund Blunden
I don't think I have ever written for anybody except the other one in oneself.

Catherine Drinker Bowen
[Over her desk hangs a yellow cardboard with the words:]
   "Will the reader turn the page?"

Anton Chekhov
When men ask me how I know so much about men, they get a simple answer: everything I know about men, I've learned from me.

Jean Cocteau
Listen carefully to first criticisms made of your work. Note just what it is about your work that the critics don't like—then cultivate it. That's the only part of your work that's individual and worth keeping.

E. E. Cummings

To be nobody-but-yourself—in a world which is doing its best, night and day, to make you everybody else—means to fight the hardest battle which any human being can fight; and never stop fighting.

Don DeLillo

I don't have a sense of a so-called ideal reader and certainly not of a readership, that terrific entity. I write for the page.

Richard Ford

A lot of people could be novelists if they were willing to devote their lives to their own responses to things.

*

[His wife Kristina is his first reader and listener.] We sit down some-place for three weeks and she goes over it line by line. As I read, she reads the line. And I say, "Does that mean what I think it means? Does that sentence sound right to you? Isn't there a beat too many in that phrase? Do you hear anything in that sentence that you don't like? Tell me what it is."

I think it probably takes the patience of a saint to be able to do that for somebody else. I mean, I know she loves me, but you get outside the bounds of love pretty fast, doing that. . . . So she has that kind of faith.

Janusz Glowacki

"Why do you write?" I was asked by an officer of the secret police in Warsaw. "An intelligent man does not write. An intelligent man does not leave any traces."

Herbert Gold

Particular life is still the best map to truth. When we search our hearts and strip our pretenses, we all know this. Particular life—we know only what we know.

Graham Greene

I write not to be read, but for my own relief. My only readership is me.

Virginia Hamilton

First, I write for myself. I want to solve something, a problem; I do that best by writing a story.

Thomas Hardy

The poet should touch our hearts by showing his own.

S. E. Hinton

I advise writing to oneself. If you don't want to read it, nobody else is going to read it.

Richard Hugo

You'll never be a poet until you realize that everything I say today and this quarter is wrong. It may be right for me, but it is wrong for you. Every moment, I am, without wanting or trying to, telling you to write like me. But I hope you learn to write like you. In a sense, I hope I don't teach you how to write but how to teach yourself to write. At all times keep your crap detector on. If I say one thing that helps, good. If what I say is of no help, let it go. Don't start arguments. They are futile and take us away from our purpose. As Yeats noted, your important arguments are with yourself. If you don't agree with me don't listen. Think about something else.

Shirley Kaufman

I will never write my poems imagining the reader. I write them for myself—to get down on paper something strongly felt which is completely unformed and undefined at the beginning. . . .

Alfred Kazin

In a very real sense, the writer writes in order to teach himself, to understand himself, to satisfy himself; the publishing of his ideas, though it brings gratifications, is a curious anticlimax.

Milan Kundera

To write a novel, you must be true to your obsessions, your ideas, and your imagination, and these are things with roots in your childhood. It is the images from your childhood and youth which form the imaginary country of your novels, and this imaginary country, in my case, is called Prague.

Margaret Laurence

One of the paradoxes of every writer is that however restrained and even reticent a person one may be—and many writers are—what you are not willing to say to your friends about your responses to life, you will declare in front of the whole world in black and white, which is absurd.

*

The first time though, I don't think of anybody. I haven't got an audience. I'm my audience, and I don't know what I'm going to discover. But once the first draft is done, I do think of potential readers, in the sense that I feel that I want to make things as clear and as effective as possible.

Doris Lessing

You have to remember that nobody ever wants a new writer. You have to create your own demand.

*

You should write, first of all, to please yourself. You shouldn't care a damn about anybody else at all. But writing can't be a way of life; the important part of writing is living. You have to live in such a way that your writing emerges from it. This is hard to describe.

John L'Heureux

The first lines of a story teach us how to read it. Tone gives us the clue. It prepares us for the story we're going to read. . . . Every story has its own rules. If it's not held together by its own blood stream, it's just self-indulgence.

Gabriel García Márquez

When I'm writing I'm always aware that this friend is going to like this, or another friend is going to like that paragraph or chapter, always thinking of specific people. In the end all books are written for your friends.

William Maxwell

I think I write for myself, and I'm astonished that strangers are moved by it.

Mekeel McBride

In early drafts, a poem is for me. After that, it's for anyone, everyone.

Arthur Miller

The writer must be in it; he can't be to one side of it, ever. He has to be endangered by it. His own attitudes have to be tested in it. The best work that anybody ever writes is the work that is on the verge of embarrassing him, always.

Czeslaw Milosz

Each of us is so ashamed of his own helplessness and ignorance that he considers it appropriate to communicate only what he thinks others will understand. There are, however, times when somehow we slowly divest ourselves of that shame and begin to speak openly about all the things we do not understand.

Marianne Moore

Any writer overwhelmingly honest about pleasing himself is almost sure to please others.

Toni Morrison

At first I wrote out of a very special place to me, although I did not understand what that place was or how to get to it deliberately. I didn't trust the writing that came from there. It did not seem writerly enough. Sometimes what I wrote from that place remained sound, even after enormous revision, but I would regard it as a fluke. Then I learned to trust that part, learned to rely on that part, and I learned how to get there faster than I had before.

V. S. Naipaul

To become a writer, that noble thing, I had thought it necessary to leave. Actually to write, it was necessary to go back. It was the beginning of self-knowledge.

Sean O'Faolain

I cannot believe that any real writer ever visualizes his readers when he is writing. He is far too busy straining to hear what his character is saying to him to have time to wonder what his reader will ultimately hear from them both.

Robert B. Parker

When I'm typing I'm not thinking about form or movie sale or audience or anything. I'm just trying to make this thing fit right, the way a carpenter likes everything square and plumb, even if it won't show. I just try to make it right for its own sake, between me and it.

Harold Pinter

When you can't write you feel you've been banished from yourself.

J. D. Salinger

Publishing is a terrible invasion of my privacy. I love to write, but I write just for myself and my own pleasure.

Margery Sharp

You must learn to write rather than be a writer. Write as well as you can. Don't think of what is wanted, what is popular, what will sell. Write what you want, and write as well as you can. . . .

Charles Simic

A good poem is about all the things you think about in the privacy of yourself.

Isaac Bashevis Singer

I don't think about an audience at all, I think about a story. I am my own first reader, and pleasing me is a hard job. If a story doesn't satisfy me, I have a good friend under my desk: the wastepaper basket.

Susan Sontag
My own view is that if you write with an audience in mind, you are involved in useless speculation. I don't believe you should think about audience. I believe you should think about *it*.

Gertrude Stein
No artist needs criticism, he only needs appreciation. If he needs criticism he is not an artist.

James Tate
I have trouble talking about audience. It's a very strange thing. I don't think people write for themselves and yet, I'm tremendously uncomfortable when suggesting I write for an audience. I don't think that this would be very original of me to say, but I write for the poem. The poem is in control. The poem, not what I'm imposing on the poem, makes the demand.

Fay Weldon
What others say are your faults, your weaknesses, may if carried to extremes be your virtues, your strengths. . . . What is weakness in small quantities, is style in overdose. So be wary of anyone who tries to teach you to write. Do it yourself. Stand alone. You will never be better than your own judgment, and you will never be satisfied with what you do. Ambition will, and should, always outstrip achievement.

Rebecca West
My skepticism long ago led me to the belief that writers write for themselves and not for their readers, and that art has nothing to do with communication between person and person, only with communication between different parts of a person's mind.

Alfred North Whitehead
A man really writes for an audience of about ten persons. Of course, if others like it, that is clear gain. But if those ten are satisfied, he is content.

other quotations that help me write:

---

other quotations that help me write:

_____

5

the writing habit

The single quality that distinguishes the unpublished writer from the published is not talent but work habits.

Writers write. That should be obvious but it isn't. That is why I have so many quotations on this issue from such a variety of writers and artists. It is hard for many young writers to understand that without discipline talent will be wasted. Writing—and the other arts—is seen as magic, not work—hard, regular, satisfying work.

I have writing friends who do not write every day, but my motto is on the wall of my writing room: *nulla dies sine linea*—never a day without a line. I have to keep the writing muscle exercised.

I also have to write every day because I never know when the writing will go or go well. Many times I think everything is just right and nothing happens; more often I think everything is wrong, it will be impossible to write, and yet when I whip myself to my writing, the writing goes well. I cannot predict when writing will arrive, so I have to be here, ready for it.

You have no idea what you have to say or how you have to say it until you put yourself in the position to receive writing. Try the writer's habit: decide that you are going to write a page, two pages, three; one hundred words, three hundred, five hundred; fifteen minutes, twenty, a half hour, an hour every day for a week. Don't judge. Accept. Try another week, then another. You'll be hooked.

But writers have secret ways they reinforce their habit. We are all a bit shamefaced about admitting our psychological—at times pathological—relationship to our craft but I keep running into other writers in stationery stores where we confess the rituals that allow us to write.

In collecting these pieces of evidence about the writer's world, even I was surprised at its eccentricity. I delight in it, revel in it, because it made my own eccentric compulsions seem normal. Well, relatively normal.

tools

The other day the poet Mekeel McBride gave me an extrafine black Pilot Varsity disposable fountain pen. She had found poems in hers, perhaps I would find some in mine. That's the way we are. A few weeks earlier I found that three other writers had ordered boxes of Pilot's extrafine black Precise V5 Rolling Ball pen. In a week, I had a dozen of my own.

Bonnie Sunstein gave me a Faber-Castell micro uni-ball, and in its black ink I have found several poems. I know the writing isn't in the brain but in the pen—and the paper. My daybooks are all versions of National's D4-33-008 ten-by-eight-inch narrow-ruled spiral notebook with green, Eye-Ease paper. I'm on my sixty-sixth daybook now, and they *must* be this size, shape, texture, especially texture. And I can't imagine how any writer can function without a beanbag desk that makes any chair or sofa into a desk. At last count our house had five of them.

Writers are becoming as obsessive about their word processors as they were about their fountain pens. When I meet with writers now, we talk of hardware and software far more often than literary fashions or even agents.

I am astonished to find myself working in an electronic office, with my own Xerox copier, IBM System 2, Model 30, with 20 mg hard disk, Hewlett Packard LaserJet Printer Series II. I even have a Hayes Smartmodem 2400 that connects me with the *Boston Globe* city room. And software: WordPerfect 5.0, Smartcom, and now the *Globe* wants me to learn Xywrite. I know I'll discover just how dependent I am on WordPerfect, how much magic there is in software.

Laugh? Go ahead. Recently I spent a month in Arizona using my IBM portable instead of this hard-disk model. I was surprised at how attached I had become to my hard disk, which so easily allows me to move around between books I am working on, poetry, columns, newsletter, novel, articles, and textbooks.

rituals

The writer is creating a world out of memory, image, imagination, specific details, facts, quotations, scenes, ideas, reports, clue, truth, questions, hints, answers, speculations, observations, shadows, reflections that are without meaning until the writer uses language to connect them.

Each morning the page is blank and the mind feels blank. To enter this world of nothingness followed by the essential chaos and confusion of our trade, the writer often depends on ritual, the artificial but tangible structures of behavior so the writer can practice the intangibles of our trade.

hours

Most writers have to find a time to write on top of working a full-time job. These hours have to come before or after the regular day's work and be woven through all the weekend chores. I wrote in the Army—some—and in school, but during the forty-one years I have been a full-time writer, I only freelanced and controlled my time for seven years and the two years since retirement.

When I worked other jobs in journalism and education, I found I had to do the writing *I* wanted to do first and that made me get up in the morning early, too early. I was angry at all lawyers, doctors, shopkeepers who did not have to pursue a job on top of a job to develop their careers. But it is not productive to go to the writing desk angry so I tried not to think of that. And when I entered the writing I escaped such matters. I was following the seductive verb, the beckoning line.

If I wrote at night, I got so excited about the writing I couldn't sleep and I didn't want to withdraw from wife and daughters. That was also true of family time weekends—and weekends weren't enough anyway, so it was the alarm before sunrise and the lonely hour when others slept.

I relish my present opportunity to write at my own pace although, ironically, the early morning habit persists. Still, writers have no time clocks, no bosses standing in the door, watch in hand. They stand each morning at the edge of a great ocean of freedom. But they soon become aware that it is easier to do anything—put out the garbage, clean the garage, drive twenty-seven miles to the stationery store, deflea the cat, even to answer what Robert Lowell called "the malignant surf of correspondence"—than to write.

I find great joy in writing but, for reasons I cannot understand, I find it hard to get to my writing desk. And once there, to write. My wife recently observed that each morning I go down to my writing desk, turn on the computer, get to the right file, put the cursor at the top left-hand corner of the blank screen, get up and go back upstairs to the bathroom.

When I return from that trip I play various games to keep me there. I have a kitchen timer and I may turn it on. I won't get up for one half hour, fifteen minutes. I'll not make tea until 10:30 on my big electric clock. Beside the screen on which I see the words I have written are *The Rules,* often not followed:

- *nulla dies sine linea.*
- Work on one project at a time.
- Write only in the morning.
- Sit. Wait. Listen. Write. Do not do *anything* else before noon.
- Lower your standards until you write "easily, quietly."
- Try to create an envelope of time in which you can write for two hours, five days a week.

For years when I was teaching, I put a parking meter on for fifteen minutes and wrote between orange juice and tea. The work piled up, the fifteen minutes added up to hours, and the pages turned into books.

words

For ten years I counted every word I wrote, yes, all the "the's" and "a's," and kept daily, weekly, monthly totals. My daughter, Hannah, no respecter of grand talent, suggested that on some days I spent more time counting words than writing them. Probably.

I stopped doing that but I have a word count on my computer, and I have been forcing myself to write three hundred words a day on one book—and the pages are piling up.

I don't remember my toilet training but anyone who has had Psych 101 can tell me about it. Yet Faulkner, Hemingway, and many others counted words, and I will continue to for two reasons:

- *Discipline:* Counting words gives me a reasonable daily goal on a long project—"You eat an elephant one bite at a time."
- *Accomplishment:* I am in no condition to evaluate the daily writing when I finish it. Writing I think is terrible, turns out to be good; writing I thought wonderful, isn't. If I count words, I can say, "Well, I did 823 words this morning" and delay their evaluation. This is especially true on a long project, when the daily stints can only be judged in the light of the entire manuscript.

places

And conditions. I can write almost anywhere that isn't quiet. The computer has made me pretty much sit in one place to write, but before the computer some of my favorite places were diners and lunchrooms or a parked car in a busy neighborhood. I begin much of my writing in my daybook that is with me all the time; but my writing is mostly done in a large basement office under our back porch that looks out on a slice of New Hampshire woods that is a far nicer view than the backside of a filling station which was my view most of my teenage years.

And I am surrounded by my toys—not only my tools but books, pictures, tapes of music, and a growing collection of CDs, classical and jazz. Here, alone, the writing comes and I am ready for it.

Woody Allen

If you work only three to five hours a day, you become quite productive. It's the steadiness that counts.

Robert Anderson

A lot of young writers wait for inspiration. The inspiration only hits you at the desk.

Jean Anouilh

I write very little, only for two hours in the morning, and then I stop even if it's going well—in fact especially if it's going well, because that's when you write those beautiful scenes like the ones in old plays, which go on and on. The next day I bring someone else into the scene and it changes.

Ahron Appelfeld

I have to work every day—it's like weaving, you have to know all the threads.

Max Apple

When things are smooth, and I can, I try to write every day. It's like physical exercise: if you miss, if you just do it once a week, it's not going to be as good as if you do it every day, four times a week, or whatever.

John Ashbery

I've conditioned myself to write at almost any time. Sometimes it doesn't work, but on the whole I feel that poetry is going on all the time inside, an underground stream.

Isaac Asimov

Rituals? Ridiculous! My only ritual is to sit close enough to the typewriter so that my fingers touch the keys.

Margaret Atwood

I have long since decided if you wait for the perfect time to write, you'll never write. There is no time that isn't flawed somehow.

Louis Auchincloss

I wrote the first draft [of *The House of Five Talents*] in longhand, with a pencil, on Saturdays, Sundays and vacations; had it typed, triple spaced; and then carried it around in a briefcase. Thus I was able to work on it very easily not only evenings but on the subway or any other time when I had a few minutes to spare. You have to be fresh for the first draft of a book, but I find that once I get to work on the second or third draft, it's like knitting.

W. H. Auden

Get up very early and get going at once, in fact, work first and wash afterwards.

J. G. Ballard

I know that if I don't write, say on holiday, I begin to feel un-settled and uneasy, as I gather people do who are not allowed to dream.

Honoré de Balzac

I am a galley slave to pen and ink.

Simone de Beauvoir

A day in which I don't write leaves a taste of ashes.

Saul Bellow

I generally write for three or four hours at a sitting, mornings as a rule. No sabbath.

Wendell Berry

After we ate I would carry a card table out into a corner of the little screened porch, and sit down to write. I would put in the morning there, conscious always as I worked of the life of the river. . . . I have never been able to work with any pleasure facing a wall, or in any other way fenced off from things. I need to be in the presence of the world.

Catherine Drinker Bowen

What the writer needs is an empty day ahead. A big round quiet space of empty hours to, as it were, tumble about in.

Gerald Warner Brace

The writer is one who writes. . . . He withdraws to some quiet corner, a bedroom perhaps, or any cubicle with a chair and table, and applies himself to his blank paper. Two hours a day are needed, three hours are better, four are heroic.

Ray Bradbury

The history of literature is the history of prolific people. I always say to students, give me four pages a day, *every day*. That's 3 or 400 thousand words a year.

John Braine

You must now draw up a timetable and stick to it. When you'll write and what rate you'll write at are a matter of individual capacity and circumstance, but I suggest that three two-hourly sessions a week are quite enough. It is essential that you record the number of words written each session. This has a valuable psychological effect: Whether you're pleased with what you've written or not, you have before you the proof that you're achieving something, that you actually are working.

Gwendolyn Brooks

The actual physical process of working with pen and paper seems to nourish my thinking.

Rosellen Brown

It's a job. It's not a hobby. You don't write the way you build a model airplane. You have to sit down and work, to schedule your time and stick to it. Even if it's just for an hour or so each day, you have to get a babysitter and make the time. If you're going to make writing succeed you have to approach it as a job. You don't wait for inspiration. The muse does not do your work for you.

Anthony Burgess

I write one page at a time—literally—and don't go on to the next one until it is finished. This habit comes from writing music.

Raymond Carver

When I'm writing, I write every day. It's lovely when that's happening. One day dovetailing into the next. Sometimes I don't even know what day of the week it is. The "paddlewheel of days" John Ashbery has called it.

Joyce Cary

Inspiration is another name for knowing your job and getting down to it.

Raymond Chandler

The important thing is that there should be a space of time, say four hours a day at least, when a professional writer doesn't do anything else but write. He doesn't have to write, and if he doesn't feel like it he shouldn't try. He can look out of the window or stand on his head or writhe on the floor, but he is not to do any other positive thing, not read, write letters, glance at magazines, or write checks. Either write or nothing. . . . Two very simple rules. A) You don't have to write. B) You can't do anything else. The rest comes of itself.

Anton Chekhov

To work and to look as though I were working, from nine in the morning till dinner, and from evening tea till bedtime, has become a habit with me, and in that respect I am just like a government clerk.

Robert Coles

I write on a quota basis. I try to write three or four yellow pages a day, five days a week. And if you keep on doing that with some—almost religious—dedication, the books mount up over the years.

Joseph Conrad

I sit here religiously every morning—I sit down for eight hours every day—and the sitting down is all. In the course of that working day of 8 hours I write 3 sentences which I erase before leaving the table in despair. . . . Sometimes it takes all my resolution and power of self-control to refrain from butting my head against the wall.

Robert Cormier

But I do not require quiet. Where I write here at home, you can see that there is no door. I've always been interested in allowing my family to be part of my work. Also, my training on the newspaper has helped me, you know, with the phones ringing, people coming and going, writing for a deadline. I write in the middle of chaos. It doesn't matter to me. I don't need solitude or seclusion to write.

Harry Crews

I get up in the morning, that's one of the hard parts, drag myself over to the old typewriter and sit down—that's even harder—and then I tell the Lord, "I ain't greedy, Lord, just give me the next 500 words."

Charles Dickens

"It is only half-an-hour"—"It is only an afternoon"—"It is only an evening," people say to me over and over again; but they don't know that it is impossible to command one's self sometimes to any stipulated and set disposal of five minutes—or that the mere consciousness of an engagement will sometimes worry a whole day.

Joan Didion

I didn't express confidence so much as blind faith that if you go in and work every day it will get better. Three days will go by and you will think every day is terrible. But on the fourth day, if you do go in, if you don't go into town or out in the garden, something usually will break through.

Annie Dillard

Writing a book is like rearing children—willpower has very little to do with it. If you have a little baby crying in the middle of the night, and if you depend only on willpower to get you out of bed to feed the baby, that baby will starve. You do it out of love.

*

I don't do housework. Life is too short and I'm too much of a Puritan. If you want to take a year off to write a book, you have to *take* that year, or the year will take you by the hair and pull you toward the grave. *Let* the grass die. I let almost all of my indoor plants die from neglect while I was writing the book. There are all kinds of ways to live. You can take your choice. You can keep a tidy house, and when St. Peter asks you what you did with your life, you can say, I kept a tidy house, I made my own cheese balls.

Lavinia Dobler

My goal is to write only one sentence a day. I write this on the bus on my way to work. I usually find that I write more than just one sentence, but ∨ the important point is that I have accomplished the goal I set by 9:00 a.m.

E. L. Doctorow

I have to write every day because, the way I work, the writing generates the writing.

*

I type single space, to get as much of the landscape of the book as possible on one page. So if I do a single space page with small margins, that's about six hundred words. If I do one page I'm very happy; that's my day's work. If I do two, that's extraordinary. But there's always a danger to doing two, which is you can't come up with anything the next day.

André Dubus

Talent is cheap. What matters is discipline.

Lois Duncan

Now I keep a typewriter with a sheet of paper in it on the end of the kitchen table. When I have a five-minute lull and the children are playing quietly, I sit down and knock out a paragraph. I have learned that I can write, if necessary, with a TV set blaring on one side of me and a child banging a toy piano on the other. I have even typed out a story with a colicky baby draped across my lap. It is not ideal—but it is possible.

John Gregory Dunne

What civilians do not understand—and to a writer anyone not a writer is a civilian—is that writing is manual labor of the mind: a job, like laying pipe.

Mignon G. Eberhart

If a day arrives when all at once I feel that to write one word is really too much to ask of any mortal, I go straight to the typewriter and write one paragraph. It is usually the wrong paragraph; and I usually have to rewrite it . . . one line or one paragraph which has been actually written is worth all the stories in the world existing in one's mind.

Epictetus

If you wish to be a writer, write.

Gustave Flaubert

I have the peculiarity of a camel—I find it difficult to stop once I get ✓ started, and hard to start after I've been resting.

*

Be regular and ordinary in your life like a bourgeois so that you may be violent and original in your work.

E. M. Forster

The act of writing inspires me.

John Fowles

But all this advice from senior writers to establish a discipline always, to get down a thousand words a day whatever one's mood, I find an absurdly puritanical and impractical approach. Writing is like eating or making love; a natural process, not an artificial one. Write, if you must, because you feel like writing; never because you feel you ought to write.

Athol Fugard

I went into a shop in Amsterdam, a very fine little shop that sells fountain pens. The old man behind the counter asked if I wanted a Parker *ball-point.* Then he began to discover I have a love for pens. He said, "Do you have Parkers and Sheaffers?" and I said, "Yes, and I also have Mont Blancs." He said, "Maybe I'll show you something." And he still hesitated. Then he went into the back room and came out with this one. He said that he had been waiting fifteen years to sell it. Pens like this are not made anymore. It's an Eversharp, and Eversharp closed up about ten years ago. It's *mint* condition; he had just refused to sell it. What a pen! An incredible pen!

One pen writes a play, and I think it's slightly adulterous if you take a pen and write another play with it. After it writes a play, it's retired from writing plays. A little delicate, modest, totally unassuming Parker, so simple it looks like nothing, wrote "Master Harold."

. . . a pen is my syringe and ink is my heroin—and a blank page is my fix every day.

John Kenneth Galbraith

All writers know that on some golden mornings they are touched by the wand—are on intimate terms with poetry and cosmic truth. I have experienced those moments myself. Their lesson is simple: It's a total illusion. And the danger in the illusion is that you will wait for those moments. Such is the horror of having to face the typewriter that you will spend all your time waiting. I am persuaded that most writers, like most shoemakers, are about as good one day as the next (a point which Trollope made).

John Galsworthy

I sink into my morning chair, a blotter on my knee, the last words or deed of some character in ink before my eyes, a pen in my hand, a pipe in my mouth, and nothing in my head. I sit. I don't intend; I don't expect; I don't even hope. Gradually my mind seems to leave the chair, and be where my character is acting or speaking, leg raised, waiting to come down, lips opened ready to say something.

Leonard Gardner

When I was working on *Fat City* I had a motto over my desk, and that was: THE ART OF THE NOVEL IS GETTING THE WHOLE THING WRITTEN. That's the most difficult thing.

Gail Godwin

I have a nice teak desk, long and wide, on which I keep special things: crisp new legal pads and No. 2 pencils with good rubber erasers that don't leave red smears; a dark blue draftsman lamp that twists and bends like a tall, limber skeleton; a small quartz clock that silently flicks the minutes; an earth-colored ceramic box in which I keep a beechnut I picked up from Isak Dinesen's grave in Denmark and a piece of rock I picked up near D. H. Lawrence's shrine in Taos, New Mexico; and an orange tomcat who lies on a blanket and snores.

I sit down facing the woods at my dark-blue typewriter, and for several hours on most mornings of my life I alternately write clusters of words slantwise on the yellow pads, then turn on the current of my typewriter and transpose them to pica type on a good grade of bond paper. I care how things look, and, with the help of the correcting tapes, even my rough drafts are clean.

Goethe

Use the day before the day. Early morning hours have gold in their mouth.

William Goldman

Writing is essentially about going into a room by yourself and doing it.

Mary Gordon

When I work, I try not to waste time. I have to write from 8:30 a.m. to 1 p.m. Then my babysitter goes home. I work outside of the house. I go to an office. I don't take phone calls. I feel I am *at work*. Discipline is in the details. You get beyond your feelings of distraction. A serious writer goes to work even when he or she doesn't want to. . . . Routine is a great grace. It's as if you don't have to invent your life. It's actually propelled by routine. You do what's expected of you.

Gunter Grass

. . . I started as a sculptor and always worked standing. I pace too, speaking each sentence aloud. Once I figured out that when I write five hours daily, I walk about 10 kilometers.

Graham Greene

If one wants to write, one simply has to organize one's life in a mass of little habits.

*

I have no talent. It's just the question of working, of being willing to put in the time.

*

I hate sitting down to work. If I don't sit down practically immediately after breakfast, I won't sit down all day. And then I don't feel guilty, but I feel depressed. I don't work for very long at a time—about an hour and a half.

*

In the old days, at the beginning of a book, I'd set myself 500 words a day, but now I'd put the mark to about 300 words.

Arthur Hailey

I set myself 600 words a day as a minimum output, regardless of the weather, my state of mind or if I'm sick or well. There must be 600 finished words—not almost right words. Before you ask, I'll tell you that yes, I do write 600 at the top of my pad every day, and I keep track of the word count to insure I reach my quota daily—without fail.

Donald Hall

In summer I'll be up at 4:30, make coffee, let out the dog, go pick up *The Boston Globe.* Then I write. First poetry. Some mornings I may not feel right and quit after 15 minutes. Other days I write poetry for a couple of hours. If I get fed up or nervous, I put it away, then work on a variety of things. I gain energy from bouncing from one thing to another, poetry to a baseball story to a children's story to a textbook. The forms are so different.

Thomas Hardy

I never let a day go without using a pen. Just holding it sets me off; in fact I can't think without it.

Ernest Hemingway

Anyone who says he wants to be a writer and isn't writing, doesn't.

*

My working habits are simple: long periods of thinking, short periods of writing.

Frank Herbert

I don't worry about inspiration, or anything like that. It's a matter of just sitting down and working . . . coming back and reading what I have produced, I am unable to detect the difference between what came easily and when I had to sit down and say, "Well, now it's writing time and now I'll write." There's no difference on paper between the two . . . you sit down and you just have conditioned yourself to: now it's writing time and you have a deadline sitting out there somewhere and you're going to do the very best you can here at this moment; and so you do it.

John Hersey

To be a writer is to sit down at one's desk in the chill portion of every day, and to write; not waiting for the little jet of the blue flame of genius to start from the breastbone—just plain going at it, in pain and delight.

Horace [Pliny, Trollope, Updike?]

nulla dies sine linea, never a day without a line

Paul Horgan

Many writers confess to observing certain professional superstitions which the non-writer would find absurd. Some break off a day's writing in mid-sentence, sure of how the sentence is to continue, so that the next day they can complete it, and thus find themselves in an already forward-moving phase of work. Others make a great fuss over having their materials arranged on their desks in exactly the same way throughout the writing of a work: the completed pages, the notes for those to come, the position of the dictionaries, the very direction of the lie of the bundle of pencils beside the typewriter, or the way the pen is pointing in its rack, the shading of the windows against sights outside too interesting to ignore, the shutting off of the telephone and the adjustment of the sense of barricade against interruption, the same sort of paper as yesterday's, the precisely repeated placing of the lamp if one has been used regularly, the condition of the fire in the fireplace, the position of an object on the chimney-piece, the re-established placing of stapler, Scotch tape, and paper clips—all these are more than matters of simple convenience or efficiency. They signify continuity. They seem like a promise that what has gone well so far will continue to do so if the proper acts of propitiation are made, and they release, in their small but powerful way, through established habit, the action of the mind which, sure of not having to arrange necessary trifles, can safely enter upon the hard but invisible work of concentration.

Samuel Johnson

If you want to be a writer, write. Write all the time.

Uwe Johnson

In this profession you have to write something every day, because language is hard to control. You have always to be keeping in touch with the contemporary way of expressing things. You have to work five hours a day, even if you just describe what your milk dealer says.

Hope Dahle Jordan

My personal, elementary rule sounds ludicrous even to me. Nevertheless, I am deadly serious when I insist it is the *only* one I conscientiously adhere to: I don't dress for the day until two pages (500 words) are written, and acceptable—to me. That is the only way I get a book finished. For as long as I stay in my blue bathrobe I stay at my typewriter.

Garson Kanin

A good plumber or a good doctor works a full eight hour day, and I don't see why a writer is any different. For the writing time of my life, I have found a scheme that is good for me. I work ten four-hour sessions a week: six full mornings, two afternoons and two evenings.

Molly Keane

I try to write for three hours in the morning, and if I don't write anything I sit and stare at the paper—otherwise, nothing would ever be written.

William Kennedy

It's hard, but I work every day—week-ends, too. I'm working on a novel set in the 19th century, and I'm more than halfway there, and every day I do something. Left foot, right foot.

Rudyard Kipling

This leads me to the Higher Editing. Take of well-ground Indian Ink as much as suffices and a camel-hair brush proportionate to the interspaces of your lines. In an auspicious hour, read your final draft and consider faithfully every paragraph, sentence and word, blacking out where requisite. Let it lie by to drain as long as possible. At the end of that time, re-read it aloud alone and at leisure. Maybe a shade more brushwork will then indicate or impose itself. If not, praise Allah and let it go, and "when thou hast done, repent not." The shorter the tale, the longer the brushwork and, normally, the shorter the lie-by, and vice-versa. The longer the tale, the less brush but the longer lie-by. I have had tales by me for three or five years which shortened themselves almost yearly. The magic lies in the Brush and the Ink. For the Pen, when it is writing, can only scratch; and the bottled Ink is not to compare with the ground Chinese stick. Experto crede.

Judith Krantz

Have some sort of private place to work in. Put up a sign to keep from being interrupted. Mine says: "PLEASE, do *not* knock, do *not* say hello or goodbye, do *not* ask what's for dinner, do *not* disturb me unless the police or firemen have to be called." It works only if I take the sign seriously *myself* and don't encourage violation of its rules. The telephone is enemy number one. Try not to have one in your work room and train your friends not to call during work hours.

Madeleine L'Engle

Inspiration usually comes during work, rather than before it.

Sinclair Lewis

Writers kid themselves—about themselves and other people. Take the talk about writing methods. Writing is just work—there's no secret. If you dictate or use a pen or type or write with your toes—it's still just work.

John MacDonald

I think the same situation is involved as painting and sculpture. If you use the best materials you can afford, somehow you have more respect for what you do with it.

Archibald MacLeish

The first discipline is the realization that there *is* a discipline—that all art begins and ends with discipline—that any art is first and foremost a craft.

*

I formed the habit long ago of putting new poems into a desk drawer and letting them lie there to ripen (or the opposite) like apples. . . . I learned early and by sad experience never to publish a green poem.

Norman Mailer

By professionalism I mean the ability to work on a bad day. . . . As you become a professional, you become more dogged. You almost have to relinquish the upper reaches of the mind to do your stint of work each day, because being a professional means being able to endure a certain amount of drudgery and the higher reaches of the mind are not enthralled by dull work.

Bernard Malamud

You write by sitting down and writing. There's no particular time or place—you suit yourself, your nature. How one works, assuming he's disciplined, doesn't matter. If he or she is not disciplined, no sympathetic magic will help. The trick is to make time—not steal it—and produce the fiction.

Thomas Mann

Even during this time [the final days of World War II] I steadfastly maintained my inveterate habit of barring out all outside impressions during the morning hours from nine to twelve or half past twelve, of reserving these hours wholly, as a matter of principle, for solitude and work.

Richard Marius

For both fiction and nonfiction, the most important part of the process is the act of writing itself. I am a compulsive writer. I not only love to write; I *must* write. If a day passes when I have written nothing, I am depressed. If I am expecting to write and something interrupts and keeps me from my task, I feel useless and lazy and somehow spent no matter what I have accomplished otherwise or how much good I may have done in another part of my working life. But several hours of writing leaves me in a state of euphoria. It may be lousy stuff. But it is *there,* and I can make it better tomorrow. I have done something worthwhile with my day.

Guy de Maupassant

Get black on white.

Larry McMurtry

Regularity is the secret. I write five pages every morning and then go down to the store. If I stick to that schedule I write quite easily and I can get through the day without feeling guilty.

John McPhee

After college, I sat all day in a captain's chair up on 84th Street trying to write plays for live television. Each morning I would thread my bathrobe sash through the spokes of the chair and tie myself in.

Peter Meinke

I think poets, like other writers, should write every day, at least a little. I rewrite poems over and over, so if nothing new seems to be coming, I put in a piece of scratch paper and begin retyping some recent poems. It's important to use scratch paper so I won't be deluded into thinking the poem is finished.

Aubrey Menen

He should sit on his bottom in front of a table equipped with writing materials. If his top end fails him, at least his nether end won't.

Henry Miller

My friend in Paris, Alfred Perles, had his own unique method. He would put his watch on the desk and say, "I'm going to write for forty-five minutes." When 45 minutes passed, he'd stop, even if it were the middle of a sentence. He was finished for the day.

Alberto Moravia

When I began my first novel, I decided to follow a precise schedule. In the morning I would "create"; in the afternoon I would "live." Since then I have always worked this way: at twelve I stop writing until the next morning at seven. By now I have made my writing an integral part of my metabolism; I write every morning just as I sleep every night and eat twice a day. This does not mean that writing is not hard work. It only means that at this stage I need to write, and if one morning I don't, I feel I am missing something. Morning is the best time; the mind after sleeping is like a white page: blank and clean.

*

I think that writing, above all, depends on behavior. I sit at the table, I arrange the light, I settle into the chair, I put a piece of paper into the typewriter.

Farley Mowat

I corner myself. I have to use great cunning to do this. I force myself into a situation where I have no alternative but to write.

Alice Munro

I still can't write if there's another adult in the house. I don't quite know why this is, but it must be that I'm still embarrassed about it somehow.

Joyce Carol Oates

When the story is more or less coherent and has emerged from the underground, then I can begin to write quite quickly—I must have done forty to fifty pages a day in *Expensive People*, though not every day. Most of the time only fifteen to twenty pages a day.

Edna O'Brien

I write in the morning because one is nearer to the unconscious, the source of inspiration.

Flannery O'Connor

Every morning between 9 and 12 I go to my room and sit before a piece of paper. Many times I just sit for three hours with no ideas coming to me. But I know one thing: If an idea does come between 9 and 12, I am there ready for it.

Robert B. Parker

There is no one right way. Each of us finds a way that works for him. But there is a wrong way. The wrong way is to finish your writing day with no more words on paper than when you began. Writers write.

*

I set myself a minimum number of pages, as a way to get from beginning, through middle, to end. The number of pages varies with circumstance. I have never set the limit lower than two pages a day, or higher than five. Unless I'm on a roll, I stop when I've written my quota.

Walker Percy

You've got to sit down and follow a schedule. Everybody's different, everybody's habits are different. I have to sit down at 9 o'clock in the morning and write for three hours or at least look at the paper for three hours. Some days I don't do *anything*. But unless you do that—punch the time clock—you won't *ever* do anything.

Reynolds Price

The day's quota for me is twenty-seven lines on a legal pad. Twenty-seven lines because twenty-seven lines add up to one typed page. I write with pen and ink, and I type it all up at the end of the week. I'm not allowed to go to bed that night until I have finished my twenty-seven-line quota for the day. And I do that six days a week until the novel or story is finished.

J. B. Priestley

Perhaps it would be better not to be a writer, but if you must, then write. You feel dull, you have a headache, nobody loves you, write. If all feels hopeless, if that famous "inspiration" will not come, write. If you are a genius, you'll make your own rules, but if not—and the odds are clearly against it—go to your desk, no matter what your mood, face the very challenge of the paper—write.

Jules Rénard

Talent is a question of quantity. Talent does not write one page; it writes three hundred.

Mordecai Richler

Well some days I find it impossible to begin, but I always spend my four hours down there and I may read magazines, I may do a crossword puzzle or check all the baseball averages or get some work done; there are days when it goes and days when it doesn't go. But I think I have to go every day in order to earn the good days.

Caryl Rivers

I enjoy the process of writing. The torment comes in getting my bottom on the chair and in front of the typewriter.

Philip Roth

I work all day, morning and afternoon, just about every day. If I sit there like that for two or three years, at the end I have a book.

Bertrand Russell

From the age of about sixteen onwards, I found the habit, in thought, of turning a sentence over and over in my mind, until I had a combination of brevity, clarity, and rhythm. . . . I wrote carefully, with many corrections, until I had passed the age of thirty, i.e. down to and including the year 1902. After that, I felt that my style was formed, for good or evil. . . . Of course, I always compose each sentence in full in my head before beginning to write it out.

Richard Selzer

Writing in longhand has a special kind of magic to it for me. You are so engaged in the manual work of fashioning the word which flows out of the end of your hand as though it were a secretion from your own body, and you watch it being spilled on the page in a certain calligraphy, and it has an energy of its own that carries you along.

Georges Simenon

From the age of seven or eight, I've been intrigued by paper, pencils, erasers, and a stationery store always fascinated me more than a candy store or a bakery. I loved the smell of it. A special kind of yellow pencil, too hard to be used in school, seemed to me more elegant, more aristocratic than anything I could think of. The same way with certain papers, for instance a drawing paper which was called, I think, Whatman paper and was used by those of my mother's boarders who were studying to be mining engineers at the university. They worked for weeks or months on the same sheet. At the end, when all the tracings were retraced with India ink (the elegance, also, of those little bottles!) they washed the much-used paper like linen.

Andrei Sinyavsky

Blank paper is an inspiration and I suggest that Balzac and Dumas wrote mountains of books because they had the good luck to own plenty of clean paper. It was there waiting for them and imposing an obligation upon them. . . . Paper exists to enable a man to forget himself and its whiteness. . . . A writer is a little like a fisherman. He sits and fishes. I may be understanding nothing, thinking nothing, but put a clean piece of paper in front of me and without fail I fish something out of it.

B. F. Skinner

I keep a cumulative record of serious time at my desk. The clock starts when I turn on the desk light, and whenever it passes twelve hours, I plot a point on a curve. I can see what my average rate of writing has been at any period. When other activities take up my time, the slope falls off. That helps me to refuse invitations.

Aleksandr Solzhenitsyn

In the camp this meant committing my verse—many thousands of lines—to memory. To help me with this I improvised decimal counting beads and, in transit prisons, broke up matchsticks and used the fragments as tallies. As I approached the end of my sentence I grew more confident of my powers of memory, and began writing down and memorizing prose-dialogue at first, but then, bit by bit, whole densely written passages. My memory found room for them! It worked. But more and more of my time—in the end as much as one week every month—went into the regular repetition of all I had memorized.

Susan Sontag

Writers, particularly prose writers, are really donkeys. You have to sit there eight hours a day—day after day after day. Poets work in shorter bouts, but for prose writers it's an extremely long, arduous task, and it's not any romantic question of inspiration. Any productive writer learns that you can't wait for inspiration. That's a recipe for writer's block.

Robert Southey

By writing much, one learns to write well.

Wallace Stegner

One of the things you have to do is simply submit to the time in front of the typewriter or desk every day. The number of hours spent writing a book is quite incredible. You write every page of every book seven or eight times—every page probably represents a day's work, at eight hours a day—and if you've got a four hundred or five hundred page book, that's thousands of hours.

*

You must submerge in a novel—or *I* must. It must be real to you as you work at it, and the only way I know to make it real is to dive into it at eight in the morning and not emerge until lunchtime. Then, for the space of each working day, it can be as real as the other life you live— the one from lunch to bedtime.

I know no way to become convinced, and stay convinced, of the reality and worthiness of a novel but to go out every morning to the place where writing is done, and put your seat on the seat of the chair, as Sinclair Lewis advised, and keep it there.

It is not an easy discipline for everyone. Young writers often rebel against it, because when they go off by themselves, day after day, they get restless.

It is the dullness of writing that they must invoke. . . .

Gertrude Stein

Any time is the time to write a poem.

John Steinbeck

When I face the desolate impossibility of writing 500 pages a sick sense of failure falls on me and I know I can never do it. Then gradually I write one page and then another. One day's work is all I can permit myself to contemplate.

Stendhal

As late as 1806 I was waiting for genius to descend upon me so that I might write. . . . If I had spoken around 1795 of my plan to write, some sensible man would have told me "to write every day for an hour or two." Genius or no genius. That advice would have made me use ten years of my life that I spent stupidly waiting for genius.

*

Vingt lignes par jour, genie ou pas. Twenty lines a day, genius or not.

David Storey

It's like working in a coal mine. I sit down to eight hours of slog a day and do a kind of shift of prose.

James Thurber

Don't get it right, get it written.

Anthony Trollope

As I journeyed across France and Marseilles, and made thence a terribly rough voyage to Alexandria, I wrote my allotted number of pages every day. On this occasion more than once I left my paper on the cabin table, rushing away to be sick in the privacy of my stateroom. It was February, and the weather was miserable; but still I did my work.

It has . . . become my custom . . . to write with my watch before me, and to requite from myself 250 words every quarter of an hour. I have found that the 250 words have been forthcoming as regularly as my watch went.

There are those who would be ashamed to subject themselves to such a taskmaster, and who think that the man who works with his imagination should allow himself to wait till inspiration moves him. . . . To me it would not be more absurd if the shoemaker were to wait for inspiration, or the tallow-chandler for the divine moment of melting. . . .

Anne Tyler

I have to begin all over every day. I get up at 6 or 6:30 to clean the house, and feed the children, and cook our supper ahead of time, so that I can be perfectly free the instant the children leave for school; but then when they're gone I find I'd rather do almost anything than go into my study. The door is so tall and dark; it looms.

The whole room smells like a carpenter's shop because of the wooden bookcases. Ordinarily, it's a pleasant smell, but mornings, it makes me feel sick. I have to walk in as if by accident, with my mind on something else. Otherwise, I'd never make it.

John Updike

I set that quota [three pages a day] for myself many years ago, and it seems to be about right. It's not so much that you're overwhelmed by it, and it's not so little that you don't begin to accumulate a manuscript.

*

For one thing, creativity is merely a plus name for regular activity; the ditchdigger, dentist, and artist go about their tasks in much the same way, and any activity becomes creative when the doer cares about doing it right, or better. Out of my own slim experience, I would venture the opinion that the artistic impulse is a mix, in varying proportions, of childhood habits of fantasizing brought on by not necessarily unhappy periods of solitude; a certain hard wish to perpetuate and propagate the self; a craftsmanly affection for the materials and process; a perhaps superstitious receptivity to moods of wonder; and a not-often-enough-mentioned ability, within the microcosm of the art, to organize, predict, and persevere.

Janwillem van de Wetering

To write you have to set up a routine, to promise yourself that you will write. Just state in a loud voice that you will write so many pages a day, or write for so many hours a day. Keep the number of pages or hours within reason, and don't be upset if a day slips by. Start again; pick up the routine. Don't look for results. Just write, easily, quietly.

Kurt Vonnegut

... novelists ... have, on the average, about the same IQs as the cosmetic consultants at Bloomingdale's department store. Our power is patience. We have discovered that writing allows even a stupid person to seem halfway intelligent, if only that person will write the same thought over and over again, improving it just a little bit each time. It is a lot like inflating a blimp with a bicycle pump. Anybody can do it. All it takes is time.

Joseph Wambaugh

I write a thousand words a day when I'm writing. Minimum. There's no deviation from that, I write a thousand words a day, every day.

Sylvia Townsend Warner

I began writing *Lolly Willowes* because I happened to find some very agreeable thin lined paper in a job lot.

Theodore Weesner

... it isn't "talent" which is so important to a writer. . . . The most important assets, I believe, are those associated with mules—a kind of stubbornness to get it done, to make it right, to make it better, and grit—not to quit—and even narrowness of purpose, a euphemism for being almost dumbly dedicated to accomplishing something.

Jessamyn West

... there are two good reasons for staying in bed. One, you have on your nightgown or pajamas and can't go running to the door at the knock of strangers. Also, once you're up and dressed, you see ten thousand things that need doing. So, I wake up and get some coffee or orange juice and go back to bed.

Morris L. West

You buy two reams—one thousand pages—of blank paper. You sit down and you write one complete page every day for one year. At the end of that time, you have a book.

E. B. White

A writer who waits for ideal conditions under which to work will die without putting a word on paper.

*

I'm glad to report that even now, at this late day, a blank sheet of paper holds the greatest excitement there is for me—more promising than a silver cloud, prettier than a little red wagon. It holds all the hope there is, all fears. I can remember, really quite distinctly, looking a sheet of paper square in the eyes when I was seven or eight years old and thinking "This is where I belong, this is it."

John Wideman

In the green woods of Maine, beside a lake, 2,200 miles from my present home in Wyoming, even farther in most ways from the cityscapes of my imagination, there is a gray wooden lawn chair perched on the edge of a dock. The setting is crucial. Like most writers, I observe rituals. A meticulously arranged scenario, certain pens, paper, a time of day, an alignment of furniture, particular clothing, coffee cooled to a precise temperature—the variations are infinite, but each writer knows his or her version of the preparatory ritual must be exactly duplicated if writing is to begin, prosper. Repetition dignifies these rituals. My return home begins with a ceremony. Early morning is my time. Bundled in a hooded sweatsuit, more a protection against mosquitoes than weather, I slouch in my gray chair at the end of the dock facing Long Lake. The morning play of water, wind and light has never been the same once in the 18 summers I've watched. From where I sit, it's almost two miles to the opposite shore. Picture a long, dark, ominous spine, low-hanging mist, white birches leaning over the water, a stillness so profound you can hear fish breaking the surface to catch insects. Whatever kind of weather they happen to be producing, the elements are always perfectly harmonized, synchronized. The trick is to borrow, to internalize for a few quiet instants, the peace of the elements at play. Whatever mood or scene I'm attempting to capture, the first condition is inner calm, a simultaneous grasping and letting go that allows me to be a witness, a mirror.

Tom Wolfe

The actual writing of a book never takes more than six months. I don't care which book it is. People who are writing on a book for five years, six years, have often said they're "writing a book." Writing a book doesn't take that long. They're doing a dance around the book. I used to do that myself. The term "work in progress" means "haven't started."

other quotations that help me write:

other quotations that help me write:

6

---

waiting for writing

fear of writing

After fifty years of writing, I have pretty much gotten over my fear of writing. Not all, but most of it. I wouldn't want to get over all of it. A little terror is stimulating. Writing is important, and you can say something that is wrong, stupid, silly, clumsy. And you will.

But there is another morning at the writing desk, another draft, another book, poem, article to write. My own fear of writing has deep roots.

I want to be loved. Oh, how I want to be loved. And we may write for that reason, but piling up verbs and nouns is not going to satisfy my—or your—insatiable hunger for appreciation. Get a dog, one with those great longing, loving looks. Imagine that they are meant for you, the real you, and not just because you are the provider of bones.

I also fear writing because I was an English major and was made to feel there was a pyramid of literature with a single manuscript at the top. And what I had to do was knock it off and place my own draft in its place.

But writing isn't playing King of the Mountain. When I sit down to write literature, all my teachers gather behind my chair and I can hear their snickers. All my classmates together with all the writers I admire, dead and alive, gather round: Chaucer, Sharon Olds, Charlie Simic, A. E. Housman, Joseph Conrad, Sue Grafton, Will Shakespeare, Chip Scanlan, Anne Tyler, Mekeel McBride, Seamus Heaney, Ross MacDonald, Robert Cormier, hundreds upon hundreds of writers.

I can't write for this crowd. I can't write literature. I can only write this page. For myself. Making it as true and as graceful as I can.

These quotations remind me that the terror is normal, that writers who are far better than I will ever be have felt it and gone on, despite the fear, to write one page at a time. And so I finish this page and turn to the next.

Spend a little time with your notebook and yourself. Identify your own particular fears, see if they are reasonable. Probably the only reasonable fear will be that you won't be able to write well enough—and that's a question that you can never answer. If you're a writer, you will have to write and put your writing in the mail. You will have to realize that some will like it, some will not. Take satisfaction in the doing—not the done.

delay or block?

The first thing to understand is there is such a thing as necessary waiting for writing. A writer drains the well with each draft, and it takes time for the well to fill. Since we are surrounded by people who mean to write (and since we were probably one of them) and never get to it, the waiting can be terrifying.

It shouldn't be. Writing goes on before the first page. The writer has to remember, observe, research, reflect, think, rehearse in a pattern that is appropriate to the project. Patience is the order of the day, even the week or month.

I used to get sick to my stomach or have a headache when I went to the desk and the writing did not come. No more. I learned that I was trying to write too soon. Now I return to my schoolroom behavior, stare out the window, watch the squirrels play follow the leader, observe a shadow as it climbs over a rock and up a tree, listen to the interplay of a string quartet, relax, let go, and then, in its own time and with its own voice, the writing comes.

Test this theory. Choose a piece of writing that you want to do but can't. Put a timer on. Sit with it for fifteen minutes—or just ten. Think about nothing else, but don't force yourself to think about the subject. Daydream. Make notes. Make a list. Stare out the window. Relax. Allow your mind to circle the subject. Play with what passes through your mind. Quit when the timer goes off.

Do this at the same time for a few days, a week, two weeks. Each session will stimulate your subconscious; you'll find yourself half-thinking about the subject during the day. Make a note: mental or in writing. If you have to do some research, do it. Then return for your fifteen- or ten-minute session the next day.

One morning you'll find you have to write. Write. Easily. Don't force it. Let it flow and stop before the well is dry, so it will flow easily the next day.

receiving writing

You have to force yourself to get your backside seated at the writing desk. That takes drive and energy, but when you are there you have to switch moods, relax, become passively aware, develop a readiness to take advantage of accident, a welcome that will invite surprise to come in, a quiet alertness that will allow you to hear the whisper of language.

Be quiet, be calm, be relaxed so that the writing may find a writer ready to receive it. Perhaps this poem of mine *(Poetry,* March 1989) will give you some practical counsel:

Waiting for a Poem

You can see the jonquil follow the sun
if you do not watch it. I spent one summer
trying to catch the tide's turn, saw it
after I left. What I did not say grows
loud in memory. My second visit to the Arctic
came between the first and second operation
when I did not wake. When I draw, my pen
reveals what I have not seen. Sometimes
I put down the telephone and walk away.
When I return I know what he has said,
and answer. At night the window reflects
what is inside. When I was fourteen,
camping in the woods, I heard the moose
charge from the lake. I knew he would
run over me and I would never suffer
his weight. Once I looked up to see
the great oak crash. I knew the surf
of leaves would fall, then rise, knew
how birds celebrate fear. Each morning
I accept the permanence of the granite
ledge outside my study window, then
when my eye followed a squirrel, high
on a branch, stepping out on air, I saw
the ledge gently rise. I hear silence
when it rises between the notes of a song,
perhaps Schubert's, perhaps Grandma's hymn
still curled in my ear. I intrude
on the privacy of roots, find my way down
into darkness, grow between rock and ledge,
seek dampness, the fellowship of worms,
the hanging on when wind sings through leaves,
and even the vast trunk bends.

Chinua Achebe

I had the key characters in my mind 15 years ago [*Anthills of the Savannah*]. I waited because the novel was not making itself available. I tried again later, and it still didn't move. I don't force things.

Margaret Atwood

The fact is that blank pages inspire me with terror. What will I put on them? Will it be good enough? Will I have to throw it out?

James Baldwin

You go into a book and you're in the dark, really. You go in with a certain fear and trembling. You know one thing. You know you will not be the same person when this voyage is over. But you don't know what's going to happen to you between getting on the boat and stepping off. And you have to trust that.

Ray Bradbury

There shouldn't *be* difficult moments. As soon as things get difficult, I turn on my heel and let the damned idea percolate on its own. I pretend to abandon it! It soon follows and comes to heel. You can't push or pressure ideas. You can't *try*, ever! You can only *do*. Doing is everything.

William Burroughs

Writer's block often results from overwriting; the general has gotten too far ahead of his army and finds his supply lines cut.

Richard Condon

I've never been blocked, but there are times when the words won't come. When I feel dried-up I deal myself a few games of solitaire at my desk. I've been doing it all my life. Sometimes I play 10 or 20 games, sometimes 40. Once, I played for three straight days. The important thing is not to leave the work place.

Robert Cormier

The blank page is there every day; that's what keeps you humble. That's what keeps your feet on the ground. No one can do it for you; and the page can be terrifyingly blank. As much as there is joy in writing, there's always the little bit of terror to keep you on edge, on your toes.

Joan Didion

I don't want to go in there at all. It's low dread every morning. That dread goes away after you've been in there an hour.

I keep saying "in there" as if it's some kind of chamber, a different atmosphere. It is, in a way. There's almost a psychic wall. The air changes. I mean you don't want to go through that door. But once you're in there you're there, and it's hard to go out.

It's a fear you're not going to get it right. You're going to ruin it. You're going to fail. The touchy part on a book—when there's not the dread in the morning, when there's the dread all day long—is before it takes. Once it takes, there's just the morning dread and the occasional three days of terrible stuff; but before it takes, there's nothing to guarantee that it's going to take.

John Gregory Dunne
Because one has written other books does not mean the next becomes any easier. Each book in fact is a tabula rasa; from book to book I seem to forget how to get characters in and out of rooms—a far more difficult task than the nonwriter might think. Still I went to my office every day. That is the difference between the professional and the amateur. The professional guts a book through this period, in full knowledge that what he is doing is not very good. Not to work is to exhibit a failure of nerve, and a failure of nerve is the best definition I know for writer's block.

Paul Engle
One of the most terrifying sights is that waiting, threatening, blank sheet. Its force is proved by the Japanese writer who, after much success, could not, for a long time, push ahead with his writing. One autumn (this is a true story) he disappeared. The next spring his body was found, after the snow had melted, high up in the mountains. Pinned to his jacket was a note only the suffering writer could have written: "I have done this because I could no longer endure the sight of the empty page."

Richard Ford
I think working on a novel is an exercise in the reassurance of belief in what you are doing. I go out to the study at 8 o'clock and by 10:30 I'm reviving the faith in what I am doing and from 11 to 12 I may get something written.

John Kenneth Galbraith
I've never sat down to write that I don't think to myself: "You'll be found out."

André Gide
It would be wisest not to worry too much about the sterile periods. They ventilate the subject and instill into it the reality of daily life.

Louise Gluck
I question the assumption behind writer's block, which is that one should be writing all the time, that at any given time there is something worthwhile to be made into a poem. We become obsessed with silence then, and fail to cultivate patience. Of course I've experienced that anxious silence we call writer's block, but at times we simply have nothing

to say. Then we need to get back in the world and put more life into
our selves.

Gail Godwin

With every long thing I write, there still comes a point where I have this
horrible hollow feeling. I think, is this interesting to anyone but me? But
then I figure, well, as long as it's burningly interesting to me, I may be
on the right track. When it starts boring me, that's when to worry.

John Irving

Henry Robbins used to call it the Enema Theory of Fiction—if you hold
off until you think you have more than you need, it will come out better.

Judith Krantz

When the great Colette was in the middle of her glorious career she
wrote to a friend, "It's terrible to think, as I do every time I start a
book, that I no longer have—that I never had—any talent . . . ."

Stanley Kunitz

Writer's block is a natural affliction. Writers who have never experienced
it have something wrong with them. It means there isn't enough friction—
that they aren't making enough of an effort to reconcile the contradic-
tions of life. All you get is a sweet, monotonous flow. Writer's block is
nothing to commit suicide over. It simply indicates some imbalance
between your experience and your art, and I think that's constructive.

Madeleine L'Engle

I got so discouraged, I almost stopped writing. It was my 12-year-old
son who changed my mind when he said to me, "Mother, you've been
very cross and edgy with us and we notice you haven't been writing. We
wish you'd go back to the typewriter."

That did a lot of good for my false guilts about spending so much
time writing. At that point, I acknowledged that I am a writer and even
if I were never published again, that's what I am.

Bernard Malamud

Teach yourself to work in uncertainty.

David Mamet

As a writer, I've tried to train myself to go one *achievable* step at a
time: To say, for example, *"Today* I don't have to be particularly inventive, all I have to be is *careful,* and make up an outline of the actual
physical things the character does in act one." And then, the following
day to say, "Today I don't have to be careful. I already have this careful,

literal outline, and all I have to do is be a little bit inventive," et cetera, et ectera.

Gabriel García Márquez

All my life I've been frightened at the moment I sit down to write.

Gregory McDonald

When an Idea for a character or a story first enters this Author's head I do my best to forget it. No, I do not make notes. Such would flatter the idea unduly. Even making *a* note would be a kind of commitment, an admittance that the soft, inept, unformed *thing* is worth a jot. . . . I do my best to forget the Idea. And if I succeed in forgetting the Idea then I conclude it deserved to be forgotten. Simple as that. The Idea is not memorable and therefore not worth developing.

Jay McInerney

I'm always afraid, when I sit down, that nothing is going to come out. That's a scary feeling when you're about to embark on a novel or short story, wondering if you're ever going to finish it, wondering how you're going to get started and what you're going to do.

Arthur Miller

I discard much more than I use, sure. I wouldn't call them blocks, though. I suppose it's simply that one is walking into the dark. When you walk in the dark, you touch objects you can't recognize, and you then have to stop and go back and walk around them from another angle.

Toni Morrison

When you first start writing—and I think it's true for a lot of beginning writers—you're scared to death that if you don't get that sentence right that minute it's never going to show up again. And it isn't. But it doesn't matter—another one will, and it'll probably be better. And I don't mind writing badly for a couple of days because I know I can fix it—and fix it again and again and again, and it will be better.

Pablo Neruda

My creatures are born of a long denial.

Joyce Carol Oates

I don't think that writer's block exists really. I think that when you're trying to do something prematurely, it just won't come. Certain subjects just need time, as I've learned over and over again. You've got to wait before you write about them.

David Rabe

Much of the early struggle in writing is with what I call "The Censor," that voice that says "It's no good" or wants to know what the third line will be before you've written the first one. That voice is very, very untalented, and when I really get going, it just vanishes.

Neil Simon

When I go to work in the morning I read the newspaper first. I don't have the slightest idea of what I'm going to do. I'm in this meditative mood. It's like being on a high board, looking down to a cold, chilly pool. Then I give myself a little push. The water isn't as cold as I thought. I don't think anyone gets writer's block. I think fear takes over.

*

I don't think I could exist without writing . . . writing is an escape from a world that crowds me. I like being alone in a room. It's almost a form of meditation—an investigation of my own life. It has nothing to do with "I've got to get another play."

Roger Simon

There is no such thing as writer's block. My father drove a truck for 40 years. And never once did he wake up in the morning and say: "I have truckdriver's block today. I am not going to work."

William Stafford

I believe that the so-called "writing block" is a product of some kind of disproportion between your standards and your performance. . . . One should lower his standards until there is no felt threshold to go over in writing. It's *easy* to write. You just shouldn't have standards that inhibit you from writing.

*

I can imagine a person beginning to feel he's not able to write up to that standard he imagines the world has set for him. But to me that's surrealistic. The only standard I can rationally have is the standard I'm meeting right now. . . . You should be more willing to forgive yourself. It doesn't make any difference if you are good or bad today; the *assessment* of the product is something that happens *after* you've done it.

Barbara Tuchman

. . . blocks (for me) generally come from difficulty of organization—that the material is resistant, or that I don't adequately understand it; it needs rethinking or additional research and a new approach.

John Updike

The terror of launching yourself into the blank paper. Nelson in this novel hang-glides, and now I see why; a writer hang-glides all the time, out over the terrible whiteness. The abyss is you, your life, your mind. It's a terrifying thing to exist at all, and an author with every creation tries to exist twice over; it is as when in poker you try to bluff a nothing hand through, and the dark face opposite raises, so you raise him back.

E. B. White

Delay is natural to a writer. He is like a surfer—he bides his time, waits for the perfect wave on which to ride in. Delay is instinctive with him. He waits for the surge (of emotion? of strength? of courage?) that will carry him along.

Tom Wolfe

What is called writer's block is always here. It's me-fear, fear that you can't do what you announced. Maybe you only announced it to few people, or only to yourself. The awful thing about the first sentence of any book is that as soon as you've written it you realize this piece of work is not going to be the great thing that you envision. It can't be.

Virginia Woolf

As for my next book, I am going to hold myself from writing it till I have it impending in me: grown heavy in my mind like a ripe pear; pendant, gravid, asking to be cut or it will fall.

other quotations that help me write:

other quotations that help me write:

7

*being found by
a subject*

We are a mercantile society, programmed to seek rather than receive. Hit the streets, pound the beat, beat the bushes, make hay while the sun . . . We are instructed to take charge, be early birds, even if we have no hunger for worms; females, as well as males, are told to get ahead, carry the ball, cross the line, score.

We are all Puritans, and we think by good work—hard, uncomfortable, unpleasant work—we shall be saved. And so we writers, like a herd of insurance salespersons, charge forth to *find the subject!*

But the best subjects are close to us; it is our individual vision of our shared, familiar world that the reader finds most informing and satisfying.

And to achieve that vision, we have to be passive, patient, observing, receptive. We do not seek but accept, an un-American, un-mercantile, un-Puritan attitude. We have to be quiet and attain a state of unthinkingness in which the material flowing in through our senses—raw and uncensored—can combine with what has been stored in memory to create the unexpected connections we call creative thinking.

If I do not have an idea for a column, would like to write a poem but do not feel the muse perched on my shoulder, or just think I should be writing about something new, I perform an exercise similar to the one I describe in chapter 2, sitting back with pen in hand and my daybook in my lap and brainstorm. I list whatever comes to mind, not forcing it, just letting details, facts, words, phrases fall on the page. Then I read to see what surprises, what connects. If nothing happens, I take a walk, go for a drive, put my feet up and stare at my woods, and ask myself questions such as the following ones. Try mine, then ask some of your own:

- What's surprised me recently?
- What's bugging me? What do I keep thinking about, what do I keep talking about?

79

- What do I appreciate that I didn't use to?
- What is changing? In me? In the world around me?
- What did I expect to happen that didn't?
- What did I not expect to happen that did?
- Why did something make me so mad? Worry me? Make me laugh? Make me sad?
- What do I keep remembering?
- What do I know that someone else needs to know?
- What do I need to know? What would I like to know? Who would I like to know?
- What do I enjoy doing?
- What needs doing? What needs to be changed?
- What have I learned?
- How is life different than I expected?
- What if . . . ?

My answers tell me what's on my mind, what's in my heart, what I have seen, felt, thought about without being aware of it. The answers tell me what I need to explore through writing.

If you do this exercise, you will *not* find THE SUBJECT. You will find many potential subjects. Pursue the seductive one, the one that is leading you on.

But pursue quietly, allowing language to lead, to flow gently though you, accepting the draft as you have accepted the material that became your subject.

Robert Anderson
Tennessee Williams says you write about what bugs you. I think you do. You write about all the concerns of the moment, or the concerns just before the moment. F. Scott Fitzgerald said that we all have had two or three things happen to us in our lives, and we go on writing about them in one way or another until people don't want to read about them anymore. The impact of my first wife's death was really quite enormous. I'm still trying to resolve it.

Margaret Atwood
Good writing takes place at intersections, at what you might call knots, at places where the society is snarled or knotted up.

Donald Barthelme
Write about what you're most afraid of.

Ann Beattie

As an artist, I'm interested in looking at the edges and seeing if they're unraveling, if they're coming apart.

Marvin Bell

One of the secrets of literature that every writer knows is that any life will do. It's not necessary to go bathe one's feet in the Ganges and travel around the world and work on a steamer to be a poet. . . . Meaning is in small things.

Saul Bellow

I blame myself for not often enough seeing the extraordinary in the ordinary. Somewhere in his journals Dostoyevsky remarks that a writer can begin anywhere, at the most commonplace thing, scratch around in it long enough, pry and dig away long enough, and, lo!, soon he will hit upon the marvelous.

Henrich Böll

If you imagine that children would really give the names of their parents to the police for political offenses, it is terrible. There's really a Shake-spearean tragedy behind such a small fact. Reading it as a note in the press, you wouldn't get that. It would be a terrible fact but you would forget about it. Yet out of that fact a writer can make a very informa-tive and true novel, one that is much more important than nonfiction. What is behind it is up to me, my imagination and my experience of the time. A writer swallows reality. There are certain kinds of fish that swallow a lot of water and plankton but need only very, very little. That's the way writers are about reality.

Vance Bourjaily

A novelist is stuck with his youth. We spend it without paying much attention to how it will work out as material; nevertheless, we must draw on whatever was there for the rest of our lives.

Albert Camus

A man's work is nothing but the slow trek to rediscover, through the detours of art, those two or three great and simple images in whose presence his heart first opened.

Raymond Carver

There's the story "A Serious Talk." That story had its genesis in a single line: "That's the last holiday you'll ever ruin for us." That line is in the story, somewhere. We all have had or seen holidays ruined in some way or another, through a family altercation or something. Once I was riding on a plane and I saw, as we were coming down, the man sitting next to me take the wedding ring off his finger and put it into his pocket. All I had to do was to imagine what might be happening there, what might be going through his mind, or what he was up to, to give me the idea for a story.

*

All of my stories have in some way to do with my own life. . . . It's a process of connections. Things begin to connect up. A line here. A word there. Stuff I heard or saw when I was 16 years old or 40 years old.

Eleanor Clark

I never begin a story with an *idea*. In fact, I like to quote the Yeats line, "Ideas rob a man of his imagination."

Robert Cormier

What if? What if? My mind raced, and my emotions kept pace at the sidelines, the way it always happens when a story idea arrives, like a small explosion of thought and feeling. What if? What if an incident like that in the park had been crucial to a relationship between father and daughter? What would make it crucial? Well, what if the father, say, was divorced from the child's mother and the incident happened during one of his visiting days? And what if . . .

*

Sometimes when there's nothing that's compelling, I do exercises. So I put a boy on a bike and had him take off on a Wednesday morning with a box on his bike. Then right away I wondered, what's he doing out of school on a Wednesday morning, where's he going, what's in the package? . . . I started to give him a lot of my own fears, phobias. . . . And I wrote virtually all of the bike part without knowing where it was going.

Roald Dahl

[Note that led to *Charlie and the Chocolate Factory:*] What about a chocolate factory that makes fantastic and marvelous things—with a crazy man running it?

Joan Didion

A young woman with long hair and a short white halter dress walks through the casino at the Riviera in Las Vegas at one in the morning. She crosses the casino alone and picks up a house telephone. I watch her because I have heard her paged, and recognize her name: she is a minor actress I see around Los Angeles from time to time, in places like Jax and once in a gynecologist's office in Beverly Hills Clinic, but have never met. I know nothing about her. Who is paging her? Why is she

here to be paged? How exactly did she come to this? It was precisely
this moment in Las Vegas that made *Play It As It Lays* begin to tell itself
to me, but the moment appears in the novel only obliquely, in a chapter
which begins: Maria made a list of things she would never do. She
would never walk through the Sands or Caesar's alone after midnight.
She would never: ball at a party, do S-M unless she wanted to, borrow
furs from Abe Lipsey, deal. She would never: carry a Yorkshire in Beverly Hills.

Alan Dugan

I'm still doing business at the same old stand—love, work, war, death,
what the world is like outside this window tonight.

John Gregory Dunne

The point of a notebook is to jump-start the mind.

Deborah Eisenberg

I have very, very little to start with. The way I start I've found there will
be maybe a phrase that just rings in my ear, maybe a sort of idiotic
phrase that stays with me, or maybe a very simple image, or a sort of
feeling, and maybe in the process of writing, the phrase or the image or
the feeling disappears or gives way, and you're not left at the end with
the thing that instigated it all. For me, most writing consists of siphoning out useless pre-story matter, cutting and cutting and cutting, what
seems to be endless rewriting, and what is entailed in all that is
patience, and waiting, and false starts, and dead ends, and really, in a
way, nerve.

James Emanuel

Whenever the special images and phrases that are always criss-crossing
in a poet's mind begin to stream in a common direction rhythmically
and distinctly, he will begin to write a poem wherever he is, or he will
try to fix the new lines in his memory until pencil and paper are available.

Paul Engle

. . . there is no such thing as material by itself, apart from the way in
which a person sees it, feels toward it, and is able to give it organized
form and expression in words . . . form is part of content, affecting it,
realizing it. A man may go through the most dramatic and horrible
experiences in war, but actually draw out of them less "material" for
writing than shy Emily Dickinson in the second-floor room of an
Amherst house, lowering notes in baskets out the window and thinking
gently of death. . . .

William Faulkner

The Sound and the Fury began with a mental picture. I didn't realize at the time it was symbolical. The picture was of the muddy seat of a little girl's drawers in a pear tree, where she could see through a window where her grandmother's funeral was taking place and report what was happening to her brothers on the ground below. By the time I explained who they were and what they were doing and how her pants got muddy, I realized it would be impossible to get all of it into a short story and that it would have to be a book. And then I realized the symbolism of the soiled pants, and that image was replaced by one of the fatherless and motherless girl climbing down the rainpipe to escape from the only home she had, where she had never been offered love or affection or understanding.

F. Scott Fitzgerald

Mostly, we authors must repeat ourselves—that's the truth. We have two or three great moving experiences in our lives—experiences so great and moving that it doesn't seem at the time that anyone else has been caught up and pounded and dazzled and astonished and beaten and broken and rescued and illuminated and rewarded and humbled in just that way ever before.

E. M. Forster

What about the creative state? In it a man is taken out of himself. He lets down, as it were, a bucket into the unconscious and draws up something which is normally beyond his reach. He mixes this thing with his normal experience and out of the mixture he makes a work of art.

*

Only connect.

Tess Gallagher

I think the places in your life where you feel contradictory tensions, yet a rightness or at least intrigue with the way the opposites balance each other into stasis, are fertile moments for the poet. A secret lives there, and although you don't want to solve it really, you instinctually want to mark your recognition of those forces answering one another so curiously.

Mavis Gallant

I see people in a situation, and it's physical, usually with a very set picture. There was a story I published recently about French Canadians, called "The Chosen Husband." It's about two sisters and a man who is more or less chosen to marry one of them. And the first thing I saw was three women standing at a window on the ground floor and watching this poor guy come up the street who doesn't know he's being watched. And I was haunted by this, the lace curtain, three women, two young women and the older one, and he's coming up the street with this box of chocolates and they're summing him up with this coldness, and detail and accuracy. And you see it more and more vividly.

Graham Greene
Isn't disloyalty as much the writer's virtue as loyalty is the soldier's?

*

For writers it is always said that the first 20 years of life contain the whole of experience—the rest is observation.

O. Henry
Write what makes you happy.

Richard Hugo
A poem can be said to have two subjects, the initiating or triggering subject, that which starts the poem or "causes" the poem to be written, and the real or generated subject, that which the poem comes to say or mean, and which is generated or discovered in the poem during the writing.

Henry James
The power to guess the unseen from the seen, to trace the implication of things, to judge the whole piece by the pattern. . . .

Maxine Kumin
The writer is looking for the informing material.

Denise Levertov
It is a sort of vague feeling that somewhere in the vicinity there is a poem, then no, I don't do anything about it, I wait. If a whole line, or phrase, comes into my head, I write it down, but without pushing it unless it immediately leads to another one. If it's an idea, then I don't do anything about it until that idea begins to crystallize into some phrases, some words, a rhythm, because if I try to push that into being by will before the intuition is really at work, then it's going to be a very bad beginning, and perhaps I'm going to lose the poem altogether. . . . You can smell the poem before you can see it. Like some animal.

Philip Levine
I was lying in bed one morning—I have very good hearing—it had been storming, and I'd usually wake up in rough weather and hear the sea,

which I lived about a half a mile from. There'd been terrific storms when I'd gone to bed. When I woke it was very quiet and calm. I listened carefully, the sea wasn't crashing on the shore, and suddenly I heard a crow—it flew over—I heard this single caw of the crow. That's the way the last part of the poem begins: "a single crow passed. . . . ' I just sort of got that in my mind, and the thing began to reach out. It was one of those times you know you're going to write a poem, and it's going to be a poem that's going to carry a lot of yourself.

Gabriel García Márquez

I suppose that some writers begin with a phrase, an idea, or a concept. I always begin with an image. The starting point of *Leaf Storm* is an old man taking his grandson to a funeral, in *No One Writes to the Colonel* it's an old man waiting, and in *One Hundred Years*, an old man taking his grandson to the fair to find out what ice is.

Mekeel McBride

I get pieces, flashes of an idea, an image, and I won't know what it means, but I'll be fascinated by it. It's all there in that first instant—it's complete—but all I know is the wonder and the curiosity. I have to make myself conscious of what the story is, what the wonder is.

You look out the window, and you see the tip of a tiger outside, and you know there's a whole tiger attached to that tip, and you wonder about the tiger: What's a tiger doing in Dover? What is the tiger like, how does it feel, what does it think? You have to track it down until you find the whole tiger. If you're really smart, you carry a pound of raw hamburger with you.

Theodore Morrison

A writer is a man walking down a street thinking how he would describe himself as a man walking down the street. . . . A novelist is someone who wonders why people act as they do, and he doesn't know, so he imagines an explanation, and that's his novel.

Joyce Carol Oates

My writing is full of lives I might have led. A writer imagines what could have happened, not what really happened.

Grace Paley

We write about what we don't know about what we know.

Marge Piercy

I think that the beginning of fiction, of the story, has to do with the perception of pattern in event. . . . At the basis of fiction is a desire to find meaningful shape in events, in the choices people make.

Katherine Anne Porter
I don't choose my stories, they choose me. Things come to my mind. Sometimes it takes years and years for them to coalesce—it's like iron filings collecting on a magnet.

Mary Lee Settle
My books have always begun with questions appearing as images, as visions.

Wallace Shawn
But usually there's nothing in front of me, just a blank space, and so that's why I don't write very much. Then, occasionally, there's a little door that opens up in the wall, and a little bit of light is glittering through the little door and I think, oh, this is a little chink in the wall, a little door, something I slightly understand and how exciting that is, how inspiring. And so I'll write about *that*.

Isaac Bashevis Singer
Writers always go back to their young days, to their young lives. If a writer writes about his life, and he is serious, he will go back there, just like a criminal goes back to the place of his crime.

William Makepeace Thackeray
The two most engaging powers of an author are to make new things familiar, familiar things new.

Virginia Woolf
. . . if there is one gift more essential to a novelist than another it is the power of combination—the single vision.

Charles Wright
The correct image is always a seed—it contains its own explanation, and defines itself. It grows and flowers of its own accord.

other quotations that help me write:

_____

other quotations that help me write:

_____

8

planning for surprise

planning

I am a writer drawn to planning and fearful of planning. I am an obsessive-compulsive—probably an untreated, acute, unapologetic, anal obsessive-compulsive—probably most writers are, note takers, list makers all. I like, no, need, to make lists; I love to make charts.

When I was an English department chairperson I would, to my wife's disgust, happily make out the teaching schedule while watching TV. It was the most fun I had in that job. When life gets to be too much—about every other week—I make a *plan*. I draw straight lines and boxes, fill in the spaces, schedule my tasks, establish priorities, write down rules I will break the next morning.

I have to plan my textbooks and their revisions. And those plans have to be shown to editors and reviewed by readers. A contract for a new textbook—and most nonfiction books—is awarded on the basis of a proposal or query, a plan. This book had to be planned. I couldn't just dump my alps of quotations on an editor, saying, "I have this huge pile of writers' quotes." I had to have a scheme, a sense of order that would serve a prospective audience.

I carefully planned this book's first two chapters again and again—one fortunately disappeared in revision and the other was revised into the foreword—and then wrote the drafts according to plan, but I couldn't plan the introductions that precede these chapters. Maybe somebody else could, but I couldn't. I had to read through the quotations and grab hold of something—the image of a wonderful smorgasbord in Norway I returned to again and again, in this case—and run with it. Now, in response to a wise editor's question, the smorgasbord is gone but not the text that was sparked by it. That's what happens to plans; they get changed by doing.

I can't plan my newspaper columns that are personal narrative essays. I have to have a line—a fragment of language that usually has an intriguing tension or contradiction within it. And then I freewrite, exploring that tension.

I can't plan a poem. This morning I came down to write this chapter but first wrote a poem. I had weighed the morning sunlight during my walk and I had to deal with that. Then I turned to this chapter and discovered I was writing a poem based on a drawing class I had visited half a dozen years ago. Later the lightness of morning sun compared to the heaviness of evening sun led me to a poem on a marriage:

Instruction by Marriage
I measure the weight of morning sun.
It was just as she expected, lighter
than in the evening. The weight grows
in color from the quiet of the day.
She taught the decibels of silence,
the geometry of turning away, staying
outside the door, watching from across
the street. She knew distance is not
between is and is but is and what could
have been. Memories are stories
more true than fact, dreams predict
and now I touch what is not there, taste
what has not yet been served, laugh
at what she will say, know the news
before the paper prints, hear, between
the words, all her choices, know at last
when it is kindness to avoid, wisdom
to leave alone. She curves the border
so the blue weed joins her garden.

Poems, when they arrive, must be welcomed. I could plan a poem, but my planned poems, like planned parties, never seem to work out for me. The order poems construct within themselves is organic and associative, and it arises during the writing. Then, in revision, I have to follow the poem's plan. And yet—in art and craft there is always a yet—I write within the tradition of contemporary poetry as a reader of poetry. I have not just flung words toward the page. There is a discipline and I have employed it.

Novels seem to want a plan, and so I sometimes try to make at least a sketch before I begin, before the novel gets stuck, usually about one-third or two-thirds of the way through. But then these plans, satisfying in the making, seem rigid and restrictive and have to be ignored, although the planning must be there somewhere in the subconscious as I write "spontaneously."

I do have to make a plan for the novel revision, but then the rewrite destroys the plan. But the plan may have been necessary to cause the draft that destroys it.

And there, in that confusion, is the tension of the creative process: the force of the spontaneous pitted against the calculated, instinct against tradition, not thinking against thinking, accident against scheme.

The writer is—and should be—drawn in two directions at once and so is the text. In that tension is creativity. The writer should plan as much—as little—as necessary to launch the draft; and the writer—the text being written—should rebel as little—as much—as necessary to create a worthwhile piece of work. The amount of planning and the amount of destruction necessary to those plans will vary according to the genre, the cognitive style of the writer, and the particular writing task.

The writer uses tradition, exerts control, provides discipline, puts in, takes out, orders, reorders, uses rhetoric, diction, grammar, mechanics to express, even produce, freedom.

Freewrite an account of an experience in your life that was important to you. Read the draft and outline the plan that the piece of writing has imposed on itself. Then plan a piece of writing on the same subject from a different point of view, write it and see how the draft has departed from and developed your plan.

That is where the writing is for me: in the text's own plan or in the destruction—or reconstruction—of my plan. The best writing is neither spontaneous nor contrived but lies in the territory between the two.

Many writers would not agree, as you will see. Do what works for you. Be a planner or a spontaneouser or work the territory in between.

exploring

For all the planning, writers are surprised by what they write. At least when the writing goes well. We expect and hope for the unexpected.

This is the single most important chapter in this book. Most people—including many teachers of writing, reading, and literature—believe that thinking precedes writing, but writers know that writing *is* thinking.

I write because I will write what I do not expect to write. I cultivate surprise. I learn I know what I did not know I knew.

When I teach or run workshops with inexperienced—and sometimes experienced—writers, I get the participants to write quickly and frequently until they are writing what they do not expect to write. That is the central act of the writing process. Language leads to meaning.

What I say overlaps and repeats a great deal of what has been said before. Of course. Writing is an integrated process. When we teach, we try to break it down into separate, watertight compartments. We can't. We can, however, change the focus of our inquiry. Here I am focusing on the discovery of meaning that comes through writing.

We discover meaning through research, thought, feeling before we come to the page. If we did not have the possibility of meaning, we would not write. But that meaning is refined, developed, changed, clarified, contradicted, deserted for a new, rebellious meaning that arises in the writing.

The way the new meaning comes and its importance cannot be predicted, but those texts that surprise the reader, that force the reader to think and/or feel in a way the reader has not thought or felt before, are usually those texts in which there was a high degree of discovery for the writer during the writing. This is why I write, more than any of the other good reasons to write; to make discoveries in my drafts.

If you have not experienced that—or even if you have—sit down right now and write of an important time in your life. Write fast, not reporting what you have thought, but describing the event—or person or place. Don't worry right now about making mistakes or writing correctly; you want instructive failures, accidents, breakthroughs into new meaning.

I'm going back in my mind a vacant lot just off Wollaston Beach. Vacant lots and boarded up stores were the landscape of the depression. It was between the first grade and the sixth, 1930 to 1936, probably after 1932. It was a familiar scene. We were playing ball after school and one of the kids fathers came up the street. We saw him, saw his slow, slump shouldered walk and we knew. He'd been laid off. His son did not run to him or wave. We never did as we did when they came home from work. We turned our back, went on with the game. We allowed him his shame. Gave him as much privacy as we could. Now I can feel that shame. We could almost taste it, touch it. It wasn't that a father couldn't provide, it was deeper than that. He had no worth—his son, his children, his wife, his neighbors knew it. It was not his fault, but it was his shame. Looking back, I remember no anger and am surprised. Just defeat. Just accepting, just giving up.

An old memory seen new. I am surprised by my new perceptions of that scene. It may become a column, a story, a poem, part of my novel, or just something stored away waiting to be used in conversation, thinking, understanding, something I will observe or experience in the years ahead. I know just a bit more than I knew before I wrote that, without intent or plan, minutes ago.

Try it. Discover how writers discover.

Edward Albee

All of sudden I discover that I have been thinking about a play. This is
usually between six months and a year before I actually sit down and
start typing it out. The characters are sort of cloudy but clear at the
same time; the nature of the play is quite clear but unspecific; what is
going to happen is sort of definite but terribly imprecise. And so I think
about it on and off for between six months and a year.

*

I may not think about it for two or three weeks but all of a sudden I'll
be walking down the street looking in a window or doing whatever I do
when I walk down the street and all of a sudden, the idea of the play or
something about the play that I discover that I have already started
thinking about—something about the play will pop into my mind. It may
be something that I have never thought about before, which would suggest—and make me a very happy to think about it this way since I'm
such a lazy person—that a great deal of the work that I do, I do unconsciously, that a great deal of the play is formed when I am thinking without using the most limited part of my mind which is the conscious part.

Woody Allen

. . . planning it. That's ninety percent of the work—pacing the floor,
thinking it out, the plot and the structure. The actual writing just takes
two to three weeks. Writing it down for me is the easiest part.

Jorge Amado

I just follow where the characters lead me.

Martin Amis

Writing a novel always feels to me like starting off in a very wide tunnel—in fact it doesn't look like a tunnel at all, since it's marvellously airy
and free at the beginning, when you are assigning life to various propositions—but finishing off by crawling down a really cramped tunnel, because the
novel has set up so many demands on you. There is so little room for
manoeuvre by the end that you are actually a complete prisoner of the
book, and it is formal demands that cause all those constrictions: the
shape gets very tight by the end, and there are no choices any more.

John Ashbery

You see I am trying to discover things that I am not already conscious
of. Rather than deal with experiences from my past which are already

familiar to me, the excitement of writing poetry for me is to explore places that I have not already found. Heidegger says that to write a poem is to make a voyage of discovery.

*

. . . the content of the poem came during the writing.

Miguel Angel Asturias
The end of the novel comes as a surprise.

*

The novelist has to become a slave to his novel; it's sort of mental bureaucracy.

Margaret Atwood
. . . you don't make a decision to write poetry; *it* makes a decision to be written.

Paul Auster
I begin with a personality, rather than an idea. And the person becomes very real to me. It's almost as though I give myself up and enter into that other consciousness. It's a funny thing but I'm not actually in control of what I'm doing. I think a lot of writers feel this way. The story and the characters become so real that they lead you along. It's a matter of following them correctly and not pushing them off the track.

James Baldwin
When you're writing, you're trying to find out something which you don't know. The whole language of writing for me is finding out what you don't want to know, what you don't want to find out.

*

You go into a book and you're in the dark, really. You go in with a certain fear and trembling. You know one thing. You know you will not be the same person when this voyage is over. But you don't know what's going to happen to you between getting on the boat and stepping off. And you have to trust that.

John Barth
Much more often I start with a shape or form, maybe an image. The floating showboat, for example, which became the central image in *The Floating Opera*, was a photograph of an actual showboat I remember seeing as a child. It happened to be named *Captain Adams' Original Unparalleled Floating Opera*, and when nature, in her heavyhanded way, gives you an image like that, the only honorable thing to do is to make

a novel out of it. I have a pretty good sense of where the book is going to go. By temperament I am an incorrigible formalist, not inclined to embark on a project without knowing where I'm going. It takes me about four years to write a novel. To embark on such a project without some idea of what the landfall and the estimated time of arrival were would be rather alarming. But I have learned from experience that there are certain barriers that you cannot cross until you get to them; in a thing as long and complicated as a novel you may not even know the real shape of the obstacle until you heave in sight of it, much less how you're going to get around it. I can see in my plans that there will be this enormous pothole to cross somewhere around the third chapter from the end; I'll get out my little pocket calculator and estimate that the pothole will be reached about the second of July, 1986, let's say, and then just trust to God and the muses that by the time I get there I'll know how to get around it.

*

But one's loyalty, as William Gass says, is finally neither to oneself as Author nor to one's readers. One's loyalty is to the object—the project in the womb, excuse the metaphor. Some objects want to be terse little stories: I've written one ten words long! Some want to be novellas, that delicious, unmarketable narrative space, too long to sell to a magazine, too short to sell to a book publisher. Some want to be lean, Flaubertian novels. And some demand to be whole countries, like *Gargantua* and *Pantagruel*, or Burton's *Anatomy of Melancholy*, or the other Burton's *1001 Nights* with its crazy notes. Or Richardson's *Clarissa*, with its 537 letters compared to my meager 88. Books one can wander around in, take various tours of, enter and leave without going through customs.

*

[The idea of characters taking charge is] a lot of baloney. You hear respectable writers, sensible people like Katherine Anne Porter, say the characters just take over. I'm not going to let those scoundrels take over.

Donald Barthelme

Art is not difficult because it wishes to be difficult, rather because it wishes to be art. However much the writer might long to be in his work, simple, honest, straightforward, these virtues are no longer available to him. He discovers that in being simple, honest, straightforward, nothing much happens: he speaks the unspeakable, whereas we are looking for the as-yet-unspeakable, the as-yet-unspoken.

Writing is a process of dealing with not-knowing, a forcing of what and how. We have all heard novelists testify to the fact that, beginning a new book, they are utterly baffled as to how to proceed, what should

be written and how it might be written, even though they've done
a dozen.

At best there is a slender intuition, not much greater than an itch.
The not-knowing is not simple, because it's hedged about with prohibi-
tions, roads that may not be taken. The more serious the artist, the
more problems he takes into account, the more considerations limit his
possible initiatives.

Peter S. Beagle

I seem to write books to find out what it is I'm writing about. In each
case, with every book I've done, I've been wrong about what I thought
it was. About two-thirds of the way through, I find out what book I'm
supposed to be doing and then I go back and make it look easy. My new
book is taking me four years to find out what it's about and who's in it.

Ann Beattie

If I get to page three or four and the material hasn't shown me the
way, I don't revise, I throw it out.

Marvin Bell

I did teach myself to write mostly by abandoning myself to the language, seeing what it wanted to say to me.

Saul Bellow

I am interested neither in affirming nor denying anything. A character
has his own logic. He goes his way, one goes with him; he has some
perceptions, one perceives them with him. You do him justice; you don't
grind your own axe.

*

I don't really know what I'm going to say. In the end it's a process of
discovery, rather than of putting something in that I know beforehand.

Michael Benedikt

I work mainly by discovering, each poem being an expedition into my
unconscious.

Thomas Berger

He's my friend and he talks to me. When I'm writing him, I can't wait to
get to the typewriter and find out what he's going to say.

Wendell Berry

I think I know how to write the books I have already written—and
though I guess, wrongly no doubt, that I could now write them better

than I did—I am discomforted by the knowledge that I don't know how to write the books that I have not yet written. But that discomfort has an excitement about it, and it is the necessary antecedent of one of the best kinds of happiness.

Judy Blume

The characters don't really live in my head; they come alive as I start to write about them; then I am never sure what is going to happen. I'm always surprised.

Henrich Böll

I will write—I am not sure whether it will be a novel or a novella—about an approximately 45-year-old woman, the wife of a politician, who leaves her house between Bonn and Bad Godesberg on a foggy evening to meet her lover, also a politician. Where this will lead the woman and myself I cannot tell yet. So far, I know neither her husband nor her lover, nor any of the other characters. I will let myself be surprised.

Robert Bolt

It is not easy to know what a play is "about" until it is finished, and by then what it is "about" is incorporated in it irreversibly and it is no more to be separated from it than the shape of the statue is to be separated from the marble. Writing a play is thinking, not thinking about thinking; more like a dream than a scheme—except that it lasts six months or more, and that one is responsible for it.

Jorge Luis Borges

A famous poet is a discoverer, rather than an inventor.

Paul Bowles

I don't feel that I wrote these books. I feel as though they had been written by my arm, by my brain, my organism, but that they're not necessarily mine.

Ray Bradbury

Creativity is continual surprise.

Anita Brookner

You never know what you will learn until you start writing. Then you discover truths you didn't know existed. These books are accidents of the unconscious.

Rosellen Brown

I often feel myself following a step or two behind my characters, full of curiosity about what they're going to do next.

William Buckley

I acknowledge that I do not know exactly what I am going to say or exactly how I am going to say it.

Anthony Burgess

By the time I start writing, I have it all in my head. A couple of years ago, when I was writing *Tremor of Intent*, a parcel came from my publisher. I thought, "Ah, good, here are the proofs of *Tremor of Intent*." I was frustrated and disappointed when I realized that I had not actually written it yet.

Samuel Butler

There is no mystery about art. Do the things that you can see, they will show you those that you cannot see. By doing what you can you will gradually get to know what it is that you want to do and cannot do, and so be able to do it.

Hortense Calisher

The real surprise is afterward. When I see that the book has made its own rules. Each one in the end makes its own form.

Raymond Carver

I begin a story with an urge to write the story, but I don't know quite where it's going. Usually I'll find out what I want to say in the act of saying it.

Joyce Cary

The work of art as completely realized is the result of a long and complex process of exploration.

John Cheever

The role autobiography plays in fiction is precisely the role that reality plays in a dream. As you dream your ship, you perhaps know the boat, but you're going towards a coast that is quite strange; you're wearing strange clothes, the language that is being spoken around you is a language you don't understand, but the woman on the left is your wife.

*

I never know where my characters come from or where they are going.

*

The legend that characters run away from their authors—taking up drugs, having sex operations and becoming president—implies that the writer is a fool with no knowledge or mastery of his craft.

Carolyn Chute

[The writing process] is sort of like when you've got no electricity and you've gotten up in the middle of the night to find the bathroom, feeling your way along in the dark. I can't hardly tell you what I do because I really don't know.

Jean Cocteau

My work is finished but I have to discover it.

Robert Cormier

One of the joys of sitting down at a typewriter is finding out what's going to happen. . . . When I'm at the typewriter (or driving the car or waiting in a supermarket line) and all the time thinking of characters, I am conscious of letting them come and go, allowing them to do all sorts of things. Some have staying power, others drift off. Some are not anticipated but arrive and hang around (like Amy Hertz or Emil Janza). I don't think of them as characters in a structured novel I am writing but simply as people that I'm watching grow and change. I don't sit down at the typewriter at nine o'clock in the morning and tell myself that I must write five or ten pages by noontime. I go to the typewriter to find out, say, what is going to happen today when young Adam Farmer goes into that lunchroom in Carver, New Hampshire, and confronts those three bullies. It may take five pages or ten pages or fifteen to find out. But finding out is the peculiar joy I encounter when I'm writing, although that same finding out sometimes leads me astray and costs me countless pages that are eventually discarded.

Julio Cortázar

I recall a curious quotation from, I think, Roger Fry: A precocious child who was talented at drawing explained his method of composition by saying, "First I think and then I draw a line around my think." In the case of my stories it is the exact opposite: the verbal line that will draw them is started without any prior "think"; it is like a great coagulation, raw material that is already taking shape in the story, that is perfectly clear even though it might seem that nothing could be more confused; in this it is like the inverted signs of the dream—we have all had dreams of midday clarity that become formless shapes, meaningless masses, when we awoke. Do you dream while you are awake when you write a short story?

*

It's the characters who direct me.

Malcolm Cowley

Most novelists . . . are like the chiefs of an exploring expedition. They know who their companions are (and keep learning more about them); they know what sort of territory they will have to traverse on the following day or week; they know the general object of the expedition, the mountain they are trying to reach, the river of which they are trying to discover the source. But they don't know exactly what their route will be, or what adventures they will meet along the way, or how their companions will act when pushed to the limit.

Robert Creeley

If you say one thing it always will lead to more than you had thought to say.

Joan Didion

I don't have a very clear idea of who the characters are until they start talking.
Nota bene:
   It tells you.
   You don't tell it.

E. L. Doctorow

There are always characters in the books who do the writing. I like to create the artist and let the artist do the work.

*

I have found one explanation that seems to satisfy people. I tell them it's like driving a car at night. You never see further than your headlights, but you can make the whole trip that way.

Robert Duncan

If I write what you know, I bore you; if I write what I know, I bore myself, therefore I write what I don't know.

Ralph Waldo Emerson

Good writing is a kind of skating which carries off the performer where he would not go.

Louise Erdrich

It's almost like the story is all done, and we have to live long enough to be receptive to it.

William Faulkner

It begins with a character, usually, and once he stands up on his feet and begins to move, all I do is trot along behind him with a paper and pencil trying to keep up long enough to put down what he says and does.

Gustave Flaubert

One is not free to write this or that. One does not choose one's subject. That is what the public and the critics do not understand.

E. M. Forster

The novelist should, I think, always settle when he starts what is going to happen, what his major event is to be. He may alter this event as he approaches it, indeed he probably will, indeed he probably had better, or the novel becomes tied up and tight. But the sense of a solid mass ahead, a mountain round or over or through which the story must somehow go, is most valuable and, for the novels I've tried to write, essential.

*

When I began *A Passage to India* I knew that something important happened in the Malabar Caves, and that it would have a central place in the novel—but I didn't know what it would be.

*

Think before you speak, is criticism's motto; speak before you think is creation's.

*

How do I know what I think until I see what I say?

John Fowles

Follow the accident, fear the fixed plan—that is the rule.

Robert Frost

No surprise for the writer, no surprise for the reader. For me the initial delight is in the surprise of remembering something I didn't know I knew.

Ernest J. Gaines

A novel is like getting on a train to Louisiana. All you know at the moment is that you're getting on the train, and you're going to Louisiana. But you don't know who you're going to sit behind, or in front of, or beside; you don't know what the weather is going to be when you pass through certain areas of the country; you don't know what's going to happen South; you don't know all these things, but you know you're going to Louisiana.

William H. Gass

. . . if any person were to suffer such a birth, we'd see the skull come out on Thursday, skin appear by week's end, liver later, jaws arrive just after eating.

*

I explored this, tried that, but like an ignorant and careless gardener, I never knew what sort of seed I had sown, so I was surprised by the height of its growth, the character of its bloom.

André Gide

The bad novelist constructs his characters; he directs them and makes them speak. The true novelist listens to them and watches them act; he hears their voices even before he knows them.

Ellen Gilchrist

I have a character named Nora Jane Whittington who lives in Berkeley, California, and who has so much free will that I can't even find out from her whether the twin baby girls she is carrying belong to her old boyfriend, Sandy, or her new boyfriend, Freddy Harwood. I can't finish my new book of stories until Nora Jane agrees to an amniocentesis. She is afraid the needle will penetrate the placenta and frighten the babies.

I created Nora Jane but I have to wait on her to make up her mind before I can finish the title story of my new book. This is a fiction writer's life.

Joanne Greenberg

Your writing is trying to tell you something. Just lend an ear.

Graham Greene

Invention is a form of organization.

*

The novel is an unknown man and I have to find him.

William Hallahan

I lay out the story in blocks, like a checkerboard. Each vertical column is a time frame (Mon., Tues., last year, whatever). I assign a horizontal row to each character, who tells his version of the story in sequence, through the time frames. In that way, I can look at any time frame and see exactly what all of the characters are doing at that moment.

When I get the chart blocked out, I sit and stare at it, testing every event, every character, challenging everything. I uncover all kinds of discrepancies, and I always see ways to make the story better, ways to increase the suspense, to eliminate unnecessary characters. I might make eight or ten revised plot charts before I'm satisfied.

Edward Hannibal

I literally draw a train of linked boxes, beginning with the central event in the middle of the page, then building the Super Chief in both directions, backward to the start, forward to the end. This very mechanical process is excellent for helping you sort your material by weight, separating incident from chapter, etc. I tack the train up on the wall in front of me and write against it, or rather I act as catalyst between the living page in the typewriter and the living chart on the wall.

Jeremiah Healy

I start thinking about a story the same way I used to conceptualize a lawsuit—by deciding where I wanted to be at the end of the case and backtracking from there.

Seamus Heaney

I have always listened for poems, they come sometimes like bodies come out of a bog, almost complete, seeming to have been laid down a long time ago, surfacing with a touch of mystery. They certainly involve craft and determination, but chance and instinct have a role in the thing too. I think the process is a kind of somnambulist encounter between masculine will and intelligence and feminine clusters of image and emotion.

*

A poem always has elements of accident about it, which can be made the subject of inquest afterwards, but there is always a risk in conducting your own inquest; you might begin to believe the coroner in yourself rather than put your trust in the man in you who is capable of the accident.

Joseph Heller

With me there's very little that I do actively in choosing the subject or choosing the person or point of view. The novel comes to me as it's written. I did not sit down to write a book about World War II, and I didn't decide to put it in the third person rather than the first person. The same thing is true of all my books. The idea occurs to me as a novel, rather than as a subject, and the novel already encompasses a point of view, a tempo, a voice.

Beth Henley

I write excessive notes, character charts and outlines before I even start the dialogue. . . . I do a certain amount of dialogue a day, which I reread the next day before I go on. I look over my notes. I always write out *What is this play all about? What are you writing? What does this mean?*

George V. Higgins

I had to learn to listen to the characters and not to push them around.

S. E. Hinton

My characters always take shape first; they wander around my mind looking for something to do.

Russell Hoban

I'm at the service of the material that enters me. It takes me where it wants to go.

Eugene Ionesco

I am always surprised. I go through life perpetually astonished at every-thing that happens around me.

John Irving

I'm on a program of spending six to eight weeks plotting out chapters and scenes and then trying to write the chapter itself in four or five days—really just blow it through—and then spend six to eight weeks tinkering.

*

I believe you have constructive accidents en route through a novel only because you have mapped a clear way. If you have confidence that you have a clear direction to take, you always have confidence to explore other ways; if they prove to be mere digressions, you'll recognize that and make the necessary revisions. The more you know about a book, the freer you can be to fool around. The less you know, the tighter you get.

P. D. James

I never begin at the beginning of a novel and work right through from the first chapter to the last. I visualize the book as a series of scenes rather as if I were shooting a film. These can be written in any order depending on how I am feeling at the time. Some mornings I am attracted to dialogue, perhaps to scenes where my detective is inter-viewing suspects and there is the cut and thrust of verbal confrontation. On others I draft descriptions of people, setting, scenery, weather, atmosphere, while sometimes I feel in the mood to tackle passages of violent action or horror. Even the weather can influence me in the scenes I choose to write at a particular time.

This jigsaw method of creation means, of course, that the whole book must be meticulously planned before any work begins.

Garrison Keillor
That's not what writing is—writing what you know. You write in order
to find things out.

William Kennedy
Inch by inch, the words surprised me.

Larry L. King
The best kind of writing, and the biggest thrill in writing, is to suddenly
read a line from your typewriter that you didn't know was in you.

Stephen King
I let the fiction, I let the book, boss itself.

Maxine Kumin
I write a poem to find out what it is I want to say. It's burrowing
inward. . . .

Milan Kundera
To be a writer does not mean to present a truth, it means to *discover* a
truth.

Stanley Kunitz
A poem has secrets that the poet knows nothing of. It takes on a life
and a will of its own.

John Le Carré
I have known very few writers, but those I have known, and whom I
respect, confess at once that they have little idea where they are going
when they first set pen to paper. They have a character, perhaps two;
they are in that condition of eager discomfort which passes for inspiration; all admit to radical changes of destination once the journey has
begun; one, to my certain knowledge, spent nine months on a novel
about Kashmir, then reset the whole thing in the Scottish Highlands. I
never heard of anyone making a "skeleton," as we were taught at
school. In the breaking and remaking, in the timing, interweaving,
beginning afresh, the writer comes to discern things in his material
which were not consciously in his mind when he began. This organic
process, often leading to moments of extraordinary self-discovery, is of
an indescribable fascination. A blurred image appears; he adds a brush-
stroke and another, and it is gone; but something was there, and he will
not rest till he has captured it.

Madeleine L'Engle

I have to go where the book wants to.

Elmore Leonard

The characters audition in their opening scene—I listen to them, see how they sound. The plots develop on their own.

Denise Levertov

Form is never more than a *revelation* of content. . . . I believe content determines form, and yet that content is discovered only *in* form. Like everything living, it is a mystery. The revelation of form itself can be a deep joy; yet I think form *as means* should never obtrude, whether from intention or carelessness, between the reader and the essential force of the poem, it must be so fused with that force. For me, back of the idea of organic form is the concept that there is a form in things (and in our experience) which the poet can discover and reveal.

C. Day Lewis

First, I do not sit down at my desk to put into verse something that is already clear in my mind. If it were clear in my mind, I should have no incentive or need to write about it.

*

We do not write in order to be understood, we write in order to understand.

Ross MacDonald

I spend from three to six months or even longer working out in note-books various possible developments of my initial idea, story develop-ments not written out as stories but as synopses of possible events. I prepare life histories for my characters and I write them down so I don't forget them. At the end of six months I might decide not to do that book now but to wait for a while. Sometimes I wait as long as ten years. I think about my books constantly, the way other people think about, perhaps, their friends and relatives. I think about the people in my books. They keep coming back to me.

Norman Mailer

Once in a while your hand will write out a sentence that seems true and yet you do not know where it came from. Ten or twenty words seem able to live in balance with your experience. It may be one's nicest reward as a writer. You feel you have come near the truth.

Bernard Malamud

When I start I have a pretty well developed idea what the book is about and how it ought to go, because generally I've been thinking about it and making notes for months if not years. Generally I have the ending in mind, usually the last paragraph almost verbatim. I begin at the beginning and stay close to the track, if it is a track and not a whalepath. If it turns out I'm in the open sea, my compass is my narrative instinct, with an assist by that astrolabe, theme. The destination, wherever it is, is, as I said, already defined.

*

I'm struggling to say it as well as I can, in a way I haven't said it before. Art lives on surprise. A writer has to surprise himself to be worth reading.

Jean Malaquais
The only time I know that something is true is at the moment I discover it in the act of writing.

I write entirely to find out what I'm thinking, what I'm looking at, what I see and what it means. What I want, and what I fear. What is going on in these pictures in my mind.

William Maxwell
Undoubtedly if I knew exactly what I was doing, things would go faster, but if I saw the whole unwritten novel stretching out before me, chapter by chapter, like a landscape, I know I would put it aside in favor of something more uncertain—material that had a natural form that it was up to me to discover.

Mekeel McBride
Writing a poem is a process of discovery, and you don't know what you're going to learn about yourself or what you're going to learn about the world until you're through with that poem. I was reading it in Iowa, which is the pig capital of the world, and somebody asked me what the poem meant. I said I don't know, it's about a pig that eats this lady's apartment, and the teacher said no, it's about loneliness, clearly. Once he said that . . . I knew what it was about. So I changed the title to "Loneliness."

Mary McCarthy
Every short story, at least for me, is a little act of discovery. A cluster of details presents itself to my scrutiny, like a mystery that I will understand in the course of writing or sometimes not fully until afterward. . . . A story that you do not learn something from while you are writing it, that does not illuminate something for you, is dead, finished before you started it.

Carson McCullers
I understand only particles. I understand the characters, but the novel itself is not in focus. The focus comes at random moments which no one

can understand, least of all the author. For me, they usually follow great effort. To me, these illuminations are the grace of labor. All of my work has happened this way. It is at once the hazard and the beauty that a writer has to depend on such illuminations. After months of confusion and labor, when the idea has flowered, the collusion is Divine. It always comes from the subconscious and cannot be controlled. For a whole year I worked on *The Heart Is a Lonely Hunter* without understanding it at all. Each character was talking to a central character, but why, I didn't know. I'd almost decided that the book was no novel, that I should chop it up into short stories. But I could feel the mutilation in my body when I had that idea, and I was in despair. I had been working for five hours and I went outside. Suddenly, as I walked across a road, it occurred to me that Harry Minowitz, the character all the other characters were talking to, was a different man, a deaf mute, and immediately the name was changed to John Singer. The whole focus of the novel was fixed and I was for the first time committed with my whole soul to *The Heart Is a Lonely Hunter.*

David McCullough

To me, writing a book is a great voyage of discovery; what attracts me to a subject in part is what I *don't* know about it, what I can learn from it.

Jay McInerney

If I didn't constantly get surprised by the material and the configurations I was stumbling onto in my writing, I don't think I'd be able to keep my interest up to finish a book.

John McPhee

I want to get the structural problems out of the way first, so I can get to what matters more. After they're solved, the only thing left for me to do is tell the story as well as possible. At that point, there is no escape. I'm just dealing with words on paper.

Herman Melville

It is not down in any map: true places never are.

H. L. Mencken

There is in writing the constant joy of sudden discovery.

W. S. Merwin

The kind of writing that matters most to me is something you don't learn about. It's constantly coming out of what I don't know rather than what I do know. I find it as I go.

Arthur Miller

I have written as my character dictated, not to some style, and I think that's true of anybody who takes the art with some seriousness.

*

I'm discovering it, making up my own story. I think at the typewriter.

Wright Morris

The language leads, and we continue to follow where it leads.

Toni Morrison

I write out of ignorance. I write about the things I don't have any resolutions for, and when I'm finished, I think I know a little bit more about it. I don't write out of what I know. It's what I don't know that stimulates me. I merely know enough to get started.

*

The controlling image is useful, because it determines the language that informs the text. Once I know what the shape of the scar is, once I know that there are two patches of orange in that quilt, then I can move. Once I have the controlling image, which can also work as the metaphor—that is where the information lodges. When I know where the white space is, then I know where the broad strokes are.

Farley Mowat

I can't program what I want to write. There's a wall between my conscious and subconscious, and I have to wait until a little trap door opens. What comes out is something over which I have no control. I can use it, manipulate and shape it, but I can't consciously control it.

Iris Murdoch

Good writing is full of surprises and novelties, moving in a direction you don't expect.

Vladimir Nabokov

The greatest happiness I experience in composing is when I feel I cannot understand, or rather catch myself not understanding (without the presupposition of an already existing creation) how or why that image or structural move or exact formulation of phrase has just come to me.

V. S. Naipaul

For everything that was false or didn't work and had to be discarded, I felt that I alone was responsible. For everything that seemed right I felt I had only been a vessel. So step by step, book by book, though seeking each time only to write another book, I eased myself into knowledge. To write was to learn. Beginning a book, I always felt I was in possession of all the facts about myself; at the end I was always surprised.

Marsha Norman

You'll notice there are little pads of paper everywhere? It works for me to write down the things I want to know. Regarding a character, the progress of a scene. . . . Even before I begin to write, I will say, "These are the things I must know before I start to write." I'll simply make the list of questions. Over the course of the next couple of weeks or months I'll get the answers to those questions.

*

Once you have the beginning and the end of the play fixed, you can construct the most direct route between the two. Say you decide you want to drive from Louisville to Omaha—you have to consult a map to figure out how to get there. If you'd like to go by way of Mammoth Cave, that's fine, but is the detour worth the extra time? You may decide to take a more direct route. Because a play is very much like a piece of machinery, you can have a mechanical approach to it and it doesn't hurt a bit. Writing plays is an orderly process. It helps if you have a logical mind.

Joyce Carol Oates

My characters really dictate themselves to me. I am not free of them, really, and I can't force them into situations they haven't themselves willed. They have the autonomy of characters in a dream.

*

The appeal of writing—of any kind of *artistic* activity—is primarily the investigation of mystery.

Flannery O'Connor

A story is good when you can continue to see more and more in it, and when it continues to escape you. In fiction two and two is always more than four.

*

Imagination is a form of knowledge.

Lawrence Osgood

Writing is like exploring. . . . As an explorer makes maps of the country he has explored, so a writer's works are maps of the country he has explored.

Cynthia Ozick
The art of fiction is freedom of will for your characters.

Grace Paley
If it turns out to be a novel, then I will have wanted to write a novel.
But if it turns out to be stories, it'll turn out that that's what I wanted
to do.

Jay Parini
. . . fictional characters, for me, soon take on a life of their own. They
run with the bit between the teeth.

Harold Pinter
The thing germinated and bred itself. It proceeded according to its own
logic. What did I do? I followed the indications, I kept a sharp eye on
the clues I found myself dropping. The writing arranged itself with no
trouble into dramatic terms. The characters sounded in my ears—it was
apparent to me what one would say and what would be the other's
response, at any given point. It was apparent to me what they would
not, could not, ever, say, whatever one might wish . . . the play was now
its own world.

Luigi Pirandello
[They] went on living on their own, choosing certain moments of the
day to reappear before me in the solitude of my study and coming—
now one, now the other, now two together—to tempt me, to propose
that I present or describe this scene or that, to explain the effects that
could be secured with them, the new interest which a certain situation
could provide, and so forth. . . . [It] became gradually harder and harder
for me to go back and free myself from them. . . . They are detached
from me; live on their own; have acquired voice and movement; have by
themselves—in this struggle for existence that they have had to wage
with me—become dramatic characters, characters that move and talk
on their own initiative; already see themselves as such; have learned to
defend themselves against me.

Anthony Powell
You establish a character; then the character follows his own logic, and
what the character does, that's his doing.

Jules Rénard
The impulse of the pen. Left alone, thought goes as it will. As it follows
the pen, it loses its freedom. It wants to go one way, the pen another. It
is like a blind man led astray by his cane, and what I came to write is no
longer what I wished to write.

Adrienne Rich

Poems are like dreams; you put into them what you don't know you know.

Alain Robbe-Grillet

It is not the situation that dictates the act of murder, it is the *text*.

Edwin Arlington Robinson

Poetry is a language that tells us . . . something that cannot be said.

Judith Rossner

I went to sleep one night and when I woke up, this girl, Dawn, had entered the room. I called myself Ouija broad. I sit down and stuff just passes through my hands.

Georges Simenon

I ask myself what set of circumstances can put this man or this woman at the absolute end of himself—this, you see, fits into my theory that the novel today should be the equivalent of the Greek tragedy, man pushed to his limit.

And then I begin making notes on yellow envelopes about my character. I try to know everything about him—who his father and mother were, where he went to school. Much of this, of course, will never find its way into the book, but I feel I must know it all in the building of the character. Then one afternoon I put a small table there beside the typewriter, where tea and pipes will be laid out for me, and in the morning I start the book.

Neil Simon

You have an idea but you don't really know where it's going. You may sorta have a vision of what the play's to be like, but you don't really know what the second act is going to be about. In *Brighton Beach,* I didn't know the second act was going to open with the father's heart attack, but when I got there that's what presented itself to me. I have to surprise myself when I'm writing because I think if you know everything that's coming, and then write it out, the audience will see what's coming too.

Louis Simpson

A poet begins by losing control; he does not choose his thoughts, they seem to be choosing him.

Isaac Bashevis Singer

. . . when I sit down to write, I don't say to myself, "I am trying to show this." I don't really know what I'm going to try; I let the story work for itself.

*

A story to me must have some surprise. The plot should be such that
when you read the first page, you don't know what the second will be.
When you read the second page, you don't know what the third will be,
because this is how life is, full of little surprises.

William Stafford
For me an artist is someone who lets the material talk back. A relationship with the material is the distinction an artist has.

Wallace Stegner
We do not write what we know; we write what we want to find out.

Gertrude Stein
[I] think of the writing in terms of discovery, which is to say that creation must take place between the pen and the paper, not before in a
thought or afterwards in a recasting.

Robert Stone
You construct characters and set them going in their own interior landscape, and what they find to talk about and what confronts them are, of
course, things that concern you most.

William Styron
I felt the architecture of *Sophie* from the very beginning. I knew it
would be a fairly long book; I knew she would be a beautiful and
doomed survivor of Auschwitz and that though Auschwitz would be the
controlling metaphor, her choice would be the ultimate metaphor.

James Tate
The poem is in control. The poem, not what I'm imposing on the poem,
makes the demand.

William Makepeace Thackeray
There are a thousand thoughts lying within a man that he does not
know till he takes up the pen to write.

Paul Theroux
Any man who knows in advance what he's going to write about would
be so bored that he'll bore his readers, or he won't finish it. So I never
begin a book—or even a story, for that matter—knowing how it's
going to end, or knowing what I'll encounter along the way.

*

In travel you discover something and then go home and write about it. In fiction the discovery comes at the moment of writing. Halfway down the page you suddenly meet something unexpected. It's the surprise in writing that is the sustaining factor.

*

It may sound pompous to say so, but I feel as if what I'm writing is inevitable. I'm not so much creating a character as discovering the character that already exists. I can't make him a certain way. He is what he is.

Calvin Trillin

I do a kind of pre-draft—what I call a "vomit-out." I don't even look at my notes to write it. It says, for example, U.S. Journal, Chicago, followed by the title, and starts out, at least, in the form of a story. But it degenerates fairly quickly, and by page four or five sometimes the sentences aren't complete. I write almost the length of the story in this way. The whole operation takes no more than an hour at the typewriter, but it sometimes takes me all day to do it because I'm tired and I've put it off a bit. Sometimes I don't even look at the vomit-out for the rest of the week and I have an absolute terror of anybody seeing it. It's a very embarrassing document. I tear it up at the end of the week.

John Updike

I really begin with some kind of solid, coherent image, some notion of the shape of the book and even of its texture. The *Poorhouse Fair* was meant to have a sort of Y shape. *Rabbit, Run* was a kind of zig-zag. The *Centaur* was sort of a sandwich. I can't begin until I know the beginning and have some sense of what's going to happen between. . . . I don't make an outline or anything. I figure that I can hold the events in my head and then hope that things will happen which will surprise me, that the characters will take on life and talk. I keep a kind of loose rein on the book.

*

Writing and rewriting are a constant search for what one is saying.

Kurt Vonnegut

It's like watching a teletype machine in a newspaper office to see what comes out.

David Wagoner

For me, writing poetry is a series of bewildering discoveries, a search for something that remains largely unknown even when you find it.

Robert Penn Warren

A poem is an exploration not a working out of a theme.

*

You don't choose a story, it chooses you. You get together with that story somehow . . . you're stuck with it.

Eudora Welty

A work of fiction creates its own rules in the writing. Each story is a different challenge, a different opportunity to do something. It has a life of its own and I think you should honor that.

You do get a story to a point where it, on its own momentum, can sort of work for you. That's a mark that you are doing it right. I do think that if the story is any good, it has a life of its own, don't you? And a momentum. And it helps you and you help it sort of at the same time. I find in every story that I write it's teaching me how to work it out as I go, which is why I love to write.

Let the story arise of itself. Let it speak for itself. Let it reveal itself as it goes along.

Your material guides you and enlightens you along the way. That's how you find out what you were after. It *is* a mystery.

I write for the sake of the story. The story is everything. I am just the instrument.

*

What discoveries I've made in the course of writing stories all begin with the particular, never the general.

*

In writing, as in life, the connections of all sorts of relationships and kinds lie in wait of discovery, and give out their signals to the Geiger counter of the charged imagination, once it is drawn into the right field.

*

I'm working on something, I don't know exactly what.

Tennessee Williams

My characters make my play. I always start with them. They take spirit and body in my mind. Nothing that they say or do is arbitrary or invented. They build the play about them like spiders weaving their webs.

Tom Williams

You learn what the characters are if you pay attention. They do things valid for what they are, not for what you thought they would be.

William Carlos Williams

The first line I ever wrote came out of the blue, with no past.

A black, black cloud
flew over the sun
driven by fierce flying
rain.

The thrill. The discovery. At once, at the same instant, I said to myself,
"Ridiculous, the rain can't drive the clouds." So the critical thing was
being born at the same time.

*

The poet thinks with his poem.

other quotations that help me write:

other quotations that help me write:

other quotations that help me write:

_____

9

the beginning line

And before the first line. When I am doing a book or an article I often begin by brainstorming fifty, one hundred, one hundred fifty titles in spare moments. Each title—not label, like *A Collection of Quotations by Writers about Writing*—is a predraft that reveals the voice, the focus, the direction of the writing.

The same is true of the first line. Sometimes the first line is given—as some of these writers indicate—but many times it is not. I often have to write many first lines—twenty-five, fifty, seventy-five. I used to have my students write at least fifteen or twenty first lines for a piece of writing. It is not time wasted; in fact it makes the writing go faster because the writing has found its voice, its aim, its destination before the writer has written a paragraph, and many of the problems that would have been revealed in a draft are foreseen, avoided, or solved.

The first lines indicate different approaches to the same material; they help refine the most interesting approaches, and they provide material that often turns up at important points or at the end.

Here, for example, is one way I might work on a piece for my "Over Sixty" column in the *Boston Globe*. I want to write about how I remember the Boston I used to work in as a young teenager before World War II:

- When I drive through the glass skyscrapers of the financial district in Boston i often see through them to the old buildings and alleys where I picked up newspaper advs. a lifetime ago.
- We all have cities of memory.
- Over Sixty we often step through the calendar and visit the cities where we worked when we were young.
- The new Boston will never erase my memories of dumpy old Boston where I learned how to get a job and hold it.

119

• The Depression was a terrible time for grown men but it gave a chance for teen-agers to hold jobs they would never have in prosperous times.

• Whenever I drive across the Tobin Bridge, part of me is that skinny boy apprenticed to the world of work and men.

• I knew alleys, back doors that were forever unlocked, secret tunnels, the Boston of a bespectacled, hustling kid who ran proofs and picked up advs just before edition.

• Boston's new glass skyscrapers and fake marble lobbies may impress some, they may even call it progress but I still live in the grimy Boston of buildings dark with soot, great windows through which no light could penetrate, men in vests, eye-shades, elastic arm bands and paper cuffs to protect who knew the way of the world and could teach me if I listened and watched.

• Boston will always be the mysterious city of my teen-age years, seething with sin and possibility.

• My Boston is still a 1930's Depression city, sooty, time worn, with sin and possibility around every street corner.

• Some people are country, my wife is town and I am city, born and bred.

• Every once in a while I look through the woods outside my study and see a skinny, depression hungry kid running through a grimy alley in Boston's financial district hustling an envelope with advertising proofs back in time for the next edition.

• The Depression was a wonderfully terrible time for me. I had fear, opportunity, responsibility, competition, a mood of desperation and failure all around me. What more could a teen-ager want?

• I see myself running as a teen-ager. Not sports, messages, errands, groceries. I was running from the Depression, towards the middle class and the dream of a single-family house.

• I can still see the Boston of my youth when I dropped out of high school and went to work running messages, picking up advertisements, hustling, whistling, lucky to have a job that paid cash money.

• Some boys knew wishing holes and deer trails, I knew Boston's alleys, tunnels, ways to get through buildings by secret doors, the short cuts of a messenger in a city.

• Driving in Boston I often take a wrong turn, not because I'm lost exactly, but I've caught a glimpse of a once familiar trail I knew as an office boy in the 1930's.

• Many of us over sixty, see a Boston that doesn't exist but is more real to us than the glossy, imitation New York the developers are trying to create on the bones of our memories.

Eighteen first lines, written quickly, a minute or three each. None of these are close to being published but each is packed with its own possibility. I want to continue with them all, but I'll have to pick one or write another sparked by this list.

Try it yourself. Pick a topic with which you're familiar and, as quickly as possible, write a dozen first lines or more. Then follow one to see where it will take you.

John Ashbery

I feel the title is a very small aperture into a larger area, a keyhole perhaps, or some way of getting into the poem. . . .

Erskine Caldwell

All I ever know is the first line, the first sentence, the first page.

Raymond Carver

For several days I'd been going around with this sentence in my head: "He was running the vacuum cleaner when the telephone rang." I knew a story was there and that it wanted telling. I felt it in my bones, that a story belonged with that beginning, if I could just have the time to write it. I found the time, an entire day—twelve, fifteen hours even—if I wanted to make use of it. I did, and I sat down in the morning and wrote the first sentence, and other sentences promptly began to attach themselves. I made the story just as I'd make a poem; one line and then the next, and the next. Pretty soon I could see a story, the one I'd been wanting to write.

*

I have that opening line and then everything seems to radiate out from that line.

Joan Didion

What's so hard about the first sentence is that you're stuck with it. Everything else is going to flow out of that sentence. And by the time you've laid down the first *two* sentences, your options are all gone.

E. L. Doctorow

[Of *Billy Bathgate*] Billy just started talking and this was the way the book happened.
  [That first sentence:]

> He had to have planned it because when we drove onto the dock the boat was there and the engine was running and you could see the water churning up phosphorescence in the river,

which was the only light there was because there was no moon, nor no electric light either in the shack where the dockmaster should have been sitting, nor on the boat itself, and certainly not from the car, yet everyone knew where everything was, and when the big Packard came down the ramp Mickey the driver braked it so that the wheels hardly rattled the boards, and when he pulled up alongside the gangway the doors were already open and they hustled Bo and the girl upside before they even made a shadow in all that darkness.

The first sentence in the book gave me everything I needed . . . Billy's recklessness; his sense of wonder; his boyishness, and his ability to rhapsodize an event that was horrifying. . . . All the people were there, from the first sentence. But I didn't know where the book was going, what it was going to be.

Nora Ephron

I don't write a *word* of the article until I have the lead. It just sets the whole tone—the whole point of view. I know exactly where I'm going as soon as I have the lead.

Raymond Federman

All my books literally come to me in the form of a sentence, an original sentence which contains the entire book. *The Twofold Vibration* began with the sentence: "If the night passes quietly tomorrow he will have reached the twenty-first century and be on his way. . . ." Once I have that first sentence, I continually examine it, scrutinize it for its implications—not only of meaning, but of tone, tonality, structure, temporal twist, etc., for in fact the entire novel is already contained there.

Elizabeth Hardwick

I remember that I started writing *Sleepless Nights* because of a single line. The line was: "Now I will start my novel, but I don't know whether to call myself I or she."

Joseph Heller

I was sitting in a chair when the opening lines of *Something Happened* came to me. On Fire Island. *Catch-22* had been out for a while and was doing pretty well but wasn't near the best-seller lists. I wanted to quit my job writing promotional copy, but I had a wife and two kids to support. I wanted to do another novel but had no ideas. I was worried. Then two sentences came to me: "In the office in which I work, there are five people of whom I am afraid. Each of these five is afraid of four people." In a dream, a kind of controlled reverie, I quickly developed the characters, the mood of anxiety, the beginning, the end and most of the middle of *Something Happened*. And I knew Bob Slocum, my protagonist, intimately. Eventually, a better opening line came to me: "I get the willies when I see closed doors," and I wrote the first chapter around that line. But I kept the original to lead off the second part.

Paul Horgan

The most important sentence in a good book is the first one: it will contain the organic seed from which all that follows will grow.

Valentin Katayev

The main thing is to take a blank sheet of paper and write the first sentence. From that first sentence springs the second, by some miracle, and then the subject emerges—what the critics call the basic concept or the conception of the work.

John L'Heureux

The first lines of a story teach us how to read it. Tone gives us the clue. It prepares us for the story we're going to read. . . . Every story has its own rules. If it's not held together by its own blood stream, it's just self-indulgence.

Gabriel García Márquez

One of the most difficult things is the first paragraph. I have spent many months on a first paragraph and once I get it, the rest just comes out very easily. In the first paragraph you solve most of the problems with your book. The theme is defined, the style, the tone. At least in my case, the first paragraph is a kind of sample of what the rest of the book is going to be. That's why writing a book of short stories is much more difficult than writing a novel.

William Maxwell

I just hang over the typewriter waiting to see what is going to happen. It begins with the very first sentence. I don't will the sentence to come; I wait, as actively passive as I can possibly be.

*

The first sentence was usually a surprise to me. From the first sentence everything else followed. A person I didn't know anything about and had never known in real life—-a man who had no enemies, a girl who doesn't know whether to listen to her heart or her mind, a woman who never draws breath except to complain, an old man afraid of falling—stepped from the wings and began to act out something I must not interrupt or interfere with, but only be a witness to: a life, with the fleeting illuminations that anybody's life offers, written in sand with a pointed stick and erased by the next high tide. In sequence the tales seem to complement one another. There are recurring themes. But I did not plan it that way. I have sometimes believed that it was all merely the result of the initial waiting with an empty mind.

Larry McMurtry

I'm very superstitious about titles. Until I get the title, I don't know what kind of book I'm going to write.

John McPhee

The first part—the lead, the beginning—is the hardest part of all to write. I've often heard writers say that if you have thousands of words to choose from, after all—and only one can start the story, then one after that, and so forth. And your material—at this point—is all fresh and unused, so you don't have the advantage of being in the middle of things. You could start in any of many places. What will you choose?

It is easier to say what not to choose. A lead should not be cheap, flashy, meretricious, blaring—a great fanfare of trumpets and then a mouse comes out of its hole. Blind leads—wherein you withhold the name of the subject and reveal it after a paragraph or so—range from slightly cheap to very cheap. I used to love doing blind leads.

Leads must be sound. They should never promise what does not follow. You pick up the newspaper and read an exciting action lead about a man being gunned down in the street. Then the story turns out to be about the debt structures in Chicago banks. Leads, like titles, are flashlights that shine down into the story. Some are much longer than others. I am not just talking about the first sentence. I am talking about an integral beginning that sets the scene and implies the dimensions of the story. That might be a few hundred words. That might be 2000 words, to set the scene for a composition 50 times as long.

V. S. Naipaul

The first sentence was true. The second was invention. But together— to me, the writer—they had done something extraordinary. Though they had left out everything—the setting, the historical time, the racial and social complexities of the people concerned—they had suggested it all; they had created the world of the street.

Marsha Norman

Never go to your typewriter until you know what that first sentence is that day. It is definitely unhealthy to sit in front of a silent typewriter for any length of time. If, after you have typed the first sentence, you can't think of a second one, go read. There is only one good reason to write a play, and that is that there is no other way to take care of it, whatever it is.

Edna O'Brien

I always have the first line. Even with my very first book, *The Country Girls*, I went around with this first sentence in my head long before I sat down to write it. "I wakened quickly and sat up in bed abruptly."

Octavio Paz

I don't usually have a clear idea of what I'm going to do. Many times I feel empty, without ideas—and then suddenly the first sentence appears. Valéry used to say that the first line is a gift. It's true: we write the first line from dictation. Who presents us with that line? I don't know. In the past people believed it was the gods, the muse, God—some power outside ourselves. In the nineteenth century it was thought to be a gift from the poet's genius. But what does *genius* mean? Later on it was the unconscious, the whole poem. The poem is a development of that line: sometimes it is written against it; at others in support of it; sometimes, when the poem is finished that first line disappears.

John Steinbeck

I suffer as always from the fear of putting down the first line. It is amazing the terrors, the magics, the prayers, the straightening shyness that assails one.

Thomas Thompson

I work longer on the first paragraph than on any other in the book. Literally, I probably tear up 200 pieces of paper before I get that first paragraph in shape. That sets the mood, that sets the tone, just like a newspaper lead.

Elie Wiesel

With novels it's the first line that's important. If I have that the novel comes easily. The first line determines the form of the whole novel. The first line sets the tone, the melody. If I hear the tone, the melody, then I have the book.

other quotations that help me write:

other quotations that help me write:

10

the voice from the text

We read a written text *and hear the writer.*

And in that hearing we make the decision to stop or read on, to distrust or believe the writer, to reject or accept the writer's view of the world.

Here is the central mystery of writing for me: How can cold, passive type press ink on a page in such a way that a human voice is heard in my ear?

The content of the text is important, and no writer can produce a worthwhile text from nothing, although many try. But we rarely read to the end of a text because of content, rarely provoked to thought or action, moved to feel, by content. It is the writer's vision of that content that attracts us, holds us, influences us.

And the writer's vision comes to us through the medium of language. The way the writer uses language accomplishes the mystery of allowing us to hear a voice when we read a page. The writer creates music—intensity, pace, rhythm, melody—in words on the page, music that supports and extends the meaning of the text and that often leads the writer to meaning.

style

Traditionally we have spoken of style in writing, a word that seems both appropriate and inappropriate to me. It is appropriate in that we write in a tradition—poetic or fictional or dramatic or critical or biographical or journalistic or scholarly or belle lettres or not so belle lettres. There are external conditions that influence writing. We have to know them and use them—or work against them. I know journalistic tradition but often work against it in my newspaper column; I know textbook tradition but often work against it writing my textbooks.

Style seems limited to the external elements in writing. It implies that you can buy a style off the rack and seems to ignore the person who wears what was bought. And so I come, as many writers do, to the term "voice."

the personal voice

Voice seems the right term to describe the human qualities in style that are, to me, the most important qualities, those elements that allow a human being to speak from the page.

My writing voice is composed of many elements. When I first visited Scotland, I could understand natives with a burr so thick my wife and children could not. I hear in my own writing traces—a twist of phrase, a word, an emphasis—that are ethnic.

The voice I hear on my page is, ironically, similar to the family I have rejected or that has rejected me. We share a way of speaking as well as a funny walk. There are genetic qualities in my voice.

And environmental factors. I believe that the ugliest accent in the world is spoken in "Dawchestah" (Dorchester), a section of Boston. I grew up a few miles south of Dorchester and can hear that in my voice. I was subjected to hours—thousands of hours—of Baptist sermons. I can hear their echo on my page. I lived in the army, in Boston, New Jersey, New Hampshire, and each has left its trace in my written speech.

I have picked up touches of my wife's Kentucky voice and hear my voice in my daughters, whose voices are different from each other. And yet we are not the same; I have my own distinct pattern of voice upon the page. And my personal voice does not cover all that happens on my page.

the voice of the text

I have come to feel that "the voice of the text" best describes what actually happens. We all speak one way to grandfather in the nursing home and another to an old acquaintance at a party. We have child voices and parent voices, neighborhood voices and stranger voices, a hundred varieties of work voices, voices for friends and voices for lovers.

We combine the voice of tradition or institution, the style that encompasses external expectations and limitations with our own way of speaking.

We see the world through language and communicate what we have seen by language, our language tuned and directed by use. Personal and impersonal factors combine in a way that is appropriate to the text, to the evolving meaning of what we are discovering we are saying and appropriate to the reader to whom we want to say it.

And just how we can do this? We don't know. It comes from listening to written language—reading—and from listening to ourselves—writing. From both we learn so that we can listen to the music of the text appearing hesitantly at first and then with increasing vigor on the page.

When I teach voice at any level—from first grade to professionals on newspapers—I have everyone write something of importance to them, then read what they have read aloud. It never fails. There are texts that touch the reader and the audience grows quiet, texts that make the readers laugh, texts that make the readers respond. The diversity of voices is rich.

To develop *your* voice, the voice of your own texts, look to what you have written and are writing. Read it aloud as you write and after you have written. Note what works, what feels right to you as you do it. List those qualities and develop them. They are you, and your task, as an artist, is to bring your vision of our world to us in your own words.

Start today. Put this book down and do it now:

- Read aloud what you are writing.
- Choose one quality you hear clearly.
- Work to improve that quality.

Repeat and repeat and repeat as long as you live.

Walter Abish

I strive for imperfection, for that rawness, clumsiness, an awkwardness—which retains an energy—so hard to do. Perfection is the death of energy.

Henri Frederic Amiel

The great artist is the simplifier.

Martin Amis

Style is absolutely embedded in the way you perceive.

Jessica Anderson

It's my tone of voice. It's the writer's presence in the story.

Max Apple

I don't work with a plot or outline or anything. The voice carries it.

Isaac Babel

A sentence is born both good and bad at the same time. The whole secret lies in a deadly perceptible twist. The control handle must be warm in your hand. You must turn it only once, never twice.

James Baldwin

The hardest thing about writing, in a sense, is not writing. I mean, the sentence is not designed to show you off, you know. It is not supposed to be "look at me!" "Look, no hands!" It's supposed to be a pipeline between the reader and you. One condition of the sentence is to write so well that no one notices that you're writing.

John Barth

I admire writers who can make complicated things simple, but my own talent has been to make simple things complicated.

Thomas Berger

The only genuine problem I ever have in my work is in arriving at a style. Once I have it—or I should say "hear it"—the book writes itself.

George Bowering

I often just get a kind of tune in my head when I start writing—much more often than I get an image to take off from, or a subject to take off from, or anything like that. I get a kind of tune going, and the tune may resolve itself into a line, with words in it, and then take off from that.

William Burroughs

What exactly is "internal dialogue"? Talking to yourself. Inner speech. Subvocal speech, which actually involves movement of the vocal chords. For some reason or other, it is very hard to stop the internal dialogue. Try it. As soon as you try it you realize how difficult it is to beat. When you try to stop it, you find out that it's not you thinking the thoughts; you're being thought.

Lewis Carroll

Take care of the sounds, and the sense will take care of itself.

Raymond Carver

I think that a writer's signature should be on his work, just like a composer's signature should be on his work. If you hear a few bars of Mozart, you don't need to hear too much to know who wrote that music, and I'd like to think that you could pick up a story by me and read a few sentences or a paragraph, without seeing the name, and know it was my story.

Willa Cather

It takes a great deal of experience to become natural.

John Cheever

For me, a page of good prose is where one hears the rain.

Winston Churchill

Short words are best and the old words are best of all.

Amy Clampit

Certainly the sound is what I start out with. I write for the ear.

Charles Darwin

I never study style; all that I do is to try to get the subject as clear as I can in my own head, and express it in the commonest language which occurs to me.

Joan Didion

Dialogue, as much as anything else, reveals the character to the writer and, ultimately to the reader. I don't have a very clear idea of who the characters are until they start talking.

E. L. Doctorow

. . . it wasn't until I was able to find the voice and forget about the intention that I was able to write the book.

*

I wait until I find a narrative voice. Then I listen to that voice and start writing.

*

I don't want a style. This was something that I was trying to explain earlier, that I want the book to invent itself. I think that the minute a writer knows what his style is, he's finished. Because then you see your own limits, and you hear your own voice in your head. At that point you might as well close up shop. So I like to think that I don't have a style, I have books that work themselves out and find their own voice—their voice, not mine. So I'll have that illusion, I think—I hope—till the very end.

Ecclesiastes

Let thy speech be short, comprehending much in few words.

Nora Ephron

I was finding a personal style, a voice if you will, a way of writing that looked chatty and informal. That wasn't the hard part—the hard part was that having found a voice, I had to work hard month to month not to seem as if I were repeating myself.

Beverley Farmer

At first I used to read each story on tape to make sure that it sounded right, but I don't do that so often now. I think I can hear the inner voice without reading it aloud.

William Faulkner

The necessity of the idea creates its own style. The material itself dictates how it should be written.

Raymond Federman

I always reread a good chunk of what I have written. I read it aloud to get the tone, the voice, the timbre back in my head.

Gustave Flaubert

An author in his book must be like God in the Universe, present everywhere and visible nowhere.

Ford Maddox Ford

A good style in literature, if closely examined, will be seen to consist in a constant succession of tiny surprises.

E. M. Forster

. . . what is always provocative in a work of art: roughness of surface. While . . . [these writings] pass under our eyes they are full of dents and grooves and lumps and spikes which draw from us little cries of approval and disapproval.

John Fowles

The most difficult task for a writer is to get the right "voice" for his material; by voice I mean the overall impression one has of the creator behind what he creates.

Anatole France

D'abord la clarte puis encore la clarte, et enfin la clarte. Clarity first, last, and always.

Robert Frost

Intellectuals deal in abstractions. It's much safer that way. Writers take risks. They deal in anecdotes and parables. The Bible is written in anecdotes and parables.

*

The ear is the only true writer and the only true reader.

Mary Gordon

I hear things in a kinesthetic way. I tap into a rhythm of language to portray what I feel.

Graham Greene

I started off with the desire to use language experimentally. Then I saw that the right way was the way of simplicity. Straight sentences, no involutions, no ambiguities. Not much description, description isn't my line. Get on with the story. Present the outside world economically and exactly.

Nancy Hale
The more particular, the more specific you are, the more universal
you are.

Elizabeth Hardwick
It's all language and rhythmn and the establishment of the relation to
the material, of who's speaking, not speaking as a person exactly, but as
a mind, a sensibility.

Michael Harper
You have to shape the word, sing in dimensions, and layer the har-
monies and jurisdictions implicit in design. It's a great discovery, the
voicing of meaning.

John Hersey
The voice is the element over which you have no control: it's the sound
of the person behind the work.

John Irving
It's important to me not only to think I know what's going to happen,
but to know the tone of voice I used toward what's going to happen,
because then I know how I'm going to *feel* toward the later material.

Henry James
In art, economy is always beauty.

Samuel Johnson
Read over your compositons and, when you meet a passage which you
think is particularly fine, strike it out.

Joubert
To write well, one needs a natural facility and an acquired difficulty.

Jane Kramer
When I find the right voice for a piece, it admits play, and that's a relief,
an antidote to being pushed around by your own words. Voice that
admits "self" can be a great gift to readers. It allows warmth, concern,
compassion, flattery, shared imperfections—all the real stuff that, when
it's missing, makes writing brittle and larger than life.

Maxine Kumin
What makes good poetry for me is a terrible specificity of detail,
whether of object or of feeling. The poet names and particularizes and
thus holds for a moment in time . . . whatever elusive event he/she is

drawn to. By terrible I mean unflinching. Honest and sometimes compassionate.

Stanley Kunitz

Poetry is language surprised in the act of changing into meaning.

*

I write my poems by saying them. It's the only way I know to write. If it doesn't satisfy my ear then I know it's wrong.

Hart Day Leavitt

It is not unusual words that count but unusual combinations of usual words.

Fran Lebowitz

In conversation you can use timing, a look, inflection, pauses. But on the page all you have is commas, dashes, the amount of syllables in a word. When I write I read everything out loud to get the right rhythm.

C. S. Lewis

Always write (and read) with the ear, not the eye. You should hear every sentence you write as if it was being read aloud or spoken.

Archibald MacLeish

A poem should not mean but be.

Katherine Mansfield

It's a very queer thing how *craft* comes into writing. I mean down to details. *Par Example.* In *Miss Brill* I chose not only the length of every sentence, but even the sound of every sentence. I chose the rise and fall of every paragraph to fit her, and to fit her on the day at that very moment. After I'd written it I read it aloud—a number of times—just as one would play over a musical—trying to get it nearer and nearer to the expression of Miss Brill—until it fitted her.

Richard Marius

I still read everything aloud. I have a fundamental conviction that if a sentence cannot be read aloud with sincerity, conviction, and communicable emphasis, it is not a good sentence. Good writing requires good rhythms and good words. You cannot know whether the rhythms and the words are good unless you read them aloud. Reading aloud is also the easiest way to see that prose tracks, that it runs on smoothly from sentence to sentence, idea to idea, section to section within the larger whole. Reading aloud also makes the mind consider connotations of words and perhaps above all their relations to each other.

Somerset Maugham

I do not write as I want to; I write as I can. ✓

Mekeel McBride

I read stuff constantly out loud as I'm writing it.

Leonard Michaels

I reread the novel many times and whenever I'd spot a passage that was too well written, I'd mess it up.

Wright Morris

Voice is the presence in the style of what is most personal to the writer. Through voice, the writer is invisibly omnipresent. It might be likened to the palette of a painter, or the characteristic sound of a composer. The reader says, "Ah, Joyce!"; the observer, "Ah, Matisse!"; the listener, "Ah, Stravinsky!" The signature is apparent in the fragment. These elements of craft are not open to analysis will not explain why they charm us. To perceive the writer in his many disguises is one of the great pleasures of reading. Behind his masks we detect his own ineffable voice. All good writers have a voice, but it plays a special role in the craft of fiction, where it reassures the reader that he is getting more than information.

Toni Morrison

The part of the writing process that I fret is getting the sound without some mechanics that would direct the reader's attention to the sound. One way is not to use adverbs to describe how someone says something. I try to work the dialogue down so the reader has to hear it. When Eva in *Sula* sets her son on fire, her daughter runs upstairs to tell her, and Eva says "Is?" and you know: a) she knows what she's been told; b) she is not going to do anything about it; c) she will not have any more conversation.

Friedrich Nietzsche

The author must keep his mouth shut when his work starts to speak.

Joyce Carol Oates

Content yields to form, form to "voice." But no one knows what "voice" is; only when it is absent; when one *hears* nothing.

George Orwell

So long as I remain alive and well I shall continue to feel strongly about prose style, to love the surface of the earth, and to take a pleasure in solid objects and scraps of useless information.

*

Good writing is like a window pane.

*

A scrupulous writer, in every sentence that he writes, will ask himself at least four questions, thus: What am I trying to say? What words will express it? What image or idiom will make it clearer? Is this image fresh enough to have an effect? And he will probably ask himself two more: Could I put it more shortly? Have I said anything that is avoidably ugly?

Blaise Pascal

When we encounter a natural style we are always surprised and delighted, for we thought to see an author and found a man.

Alexander Pope

True ease in writing comes from art, not chance,
As those move easiest who have learned to dance.
'Tis not enough no harshness give offence,
The sound must seem an echo to the sense.

Katherine Anne Porter

If you have a character of your own, you will have a style of your own. . . . Your style grows as your ideas grow, and as your knowledge of your craft increases.

Marcel Proust

Style is a matter of vision, not technique.

Lillian Ross

One of the conspicuous things about Aubrey, Defoe, Turgenev, and Mayhew is that they were all enraptured by facts. They tried to set down what could be seen and heard and touched, what could be tested and confirmed by others: what was true. They wrote about particulars; they didn't generalize. They didn't analyze; they tried to understand but not overinterpret. They did not indulge in flourishes; they did not feel a need to show off. All of them wrote at times in the first person, but none of them called attention to himself.

Mary Lee Settle

Every book should have its own voice—what you hear in your head as you read to yourself.

Mark Smith

I come to a book and say "What does the book demand of me, or impose on my style, or way of looking at the world?" Somebody like

Henry James would always come to whatever he wrote with a fixed style. Probably a fixed tone, too. Each book is a new problem for me. . . . I would be very bored if I repeated myself technically, stylistically.

Robert Southey
Be brief; for it is with words as with sunbeams, the more they are con- ✓ densed, the deeper they burn.

Stendhal
I see but one rule: to be clear.

Wallace Stevens
Poetry is an abstraction blooded.

William Strunk
Vigorous writing is concise. A sentence should contain no unnecessary words, a paragraph no unnecessary sentences, for the same reason that a drawing should have no unnecessary lines and a machine no unnecessary parts. This requires not that the writer make all his sentences short, or that he avoid all detail and treat his subjects only in outline, but that every word tell.

Dylan Thomas
The best craftsmanship always leaves holes and gaps in the works of the poem so that something that is *not* in the poem can creep, crawl, flash, or thunder in.

Henry David Thoreau
As for style of writing, if one has anything to say, it drops from him simply and directly as a stone falls to the ground.

Leo Tolstoy
This indeed is one of the significant facts about a true work of art . . . that its content in its entirety can be expressed only by itself.

Barbara Tuchman
Nothing is more satisfying than to write a good sentence. It is no fun to write lumpishly, dully, in prose the reader must plod through like wet sand. But it is a pleasure to achieve, if one can, a clear running prose that is simple yet full of surprises.

John Updike
I notice that as I write it comes out as sort of Updike prose. I sit down in such different moods, wearing such different clothes, and out this comes—like a kind of handwriting. It's always mine, and there's no way I can seem to get around it. Isn't it funny you have only one voice?

Fay Weldon

I don't like too many adjectives or adverbs—I say if a noun or a verb is worth describing, do it properly, take a sentence to do it. There's no hurry. Don't say "the quick brown fox jumped over the lazy dog." Say, "it was at this moment that the fox jumped over the dog. The fox was brown as the hazelnuts in the tree hedgerows, and quick as the small stream that ran beside, and the dog too lazy to so much as turn his head." Or something. Writing is more than just the making of a series of comprehensible statements: it is the gathering in of connotations; the harvesting of them, like blackberries in a good season, ripe and heavy, snatched from among the thorns of logic.

Having thus discouraged the apprentice writer from over-use of adjectives, I turn at once to Iris Murdoch and find she will use eighteen of them in a row. It works.

Eudora Welty

Ever since I was first read to, then started reading to myself, there has never been a line read that I didn't *hear*. As my eyes followed the sentence, a voice was saying it silently to me. It isn't my mother's voice, or the voice of any person I can identify, certainly not my own. It is human, but inward, and it is inwardly that I listen to it. It is to me the voice of the story or the poem itself. . . .

My own words, when I am at work on a story, I hear too as they go, in the same voice that I hear when I read in books. When I write and the sound of it comes back to my ears, then I act to make my changes. I have always trusted this voice.

*

I never wrote a word that I didn't hear as I read.

Jessamyn West

A writer should describe reality with a touch of unreality, an element of distortion. That's the magic of creativeness. A literal transcription—a photograph—isn't enough.

E. B. White

Style results more from what a person is than from what he knows.

Elie Wiesel

Literature is a tone. It is a melody. If I find the melody of the book, the book is written. . . .

Every book has its own. It's more than simple rhythm. It's like a musical key, major or minor, but more so. If you have that key, you must know you can go on—the book is there.

Miller Williams

This forward motion is also carried by the sounds. When I write, I write out loud. It's very important to me how the consonants click off against one another and how the vowels move into one another and out again. I also like the sounds of a line to move in an interesting and logical way through the mouth.

Tennessee Williams

I do a lot of talking to myself when I write, trying out the sound of dialogue. Neighbors must think I always have a roomful of company.

William Butler Yeats

Only that which does not teach, which does not cry out, which does not condescend, which does not explain, is irresistible.

other quotations that help me write:

other quotations that help me write:

11

---

riding the flow

The longer I write, the more important I believe it is to write the first draft as fast as possible. In drafting, I push myself so I am at the edge of discomfort. There are three reasons this is important for me:

1. I feel that I am a conduit for the text. It has its own energy, its own purpose, its own direction. After the text has arrived, I can evaluate and revise it, but my job is to allow that text to arrive with as natural a birth as possible, and fastwriting helps to keep me out of the way, allows the text to develop its own momentum.
2. We all have our own censors who stand guard as we write. They want to prevent surprise, control the unexpected, reinforce tradition, halt risk while we are trying to say what hasn't been said before, not quite in the way we are in the process of saying it. Fastwriting allows me, if I am speedy, to get ahead of the censors for an hour or so. They always catch up, but my best writing comes in those moments of escape when I duck into an alley or find a place of quiet behind some trees and hear the censors gallop past.
3. I fastwrite to cause accident. Accident causes surprise and I thrive on surprise; writing what I do not expect is what happens when the writing goes well. I have to cultivate accident: the accident of connection when details that have never been related before snap together in a new meaning; when I use the wrong word or a strange combination of words that turns out to be just right; where language and fact reveal a new insight; when form and meaning indicate a new way of saying what I am learning I have to say.

Later, it will be time for consideration and reconsideration, slow, careful revision and editing. But on the first draft I have to achieve velocity, just as you do if you want the bike to balance.

Try it. Again, set a timer as a help to banish self-censorship. Don't say, "I am going to write well"; say, "I'm just going to write for half an hour." Pick tools that help you to write as easily as possible. Write fast, uncomfortably fast. What will happen? You'll produce a draft, a draft that needs work, of course, but you'll have a piece of writing. You have a specific task in front of you from which you can learn—or relearn—your craft.

Ann Beattie

If one doesn't have a momentum of its own by the fifth page it ends up in the trash.

John Braine

The more quickly you write, the better. It's of no consequence if the story doesn't seem to hang together, and though you should try to fill out the story as much as you can, it's of no consequence what you leave out.

Anthony Burgess

It's important that a novel be approached with some urgency. Spend too long on it, or have great gaps between writing sessions, and the unity of the work tends to be lost.

Raymond Carver

I write the first draft quickly, as I said. This is most often done in long-hand. I simply fill up the pages as rapidly as I can. In some cases, there's a kind of personal shorthand, notes to myself for what I will do later when I come back to it. Some scenes I have to leave unfinished, unwritten in some cases; the scenes that will require meticulous care later. I mean all of it requires meticulous care—but some scenes I save until the second or third draft, because to do them and do them right would take too much time on the first draft. With the first draft it's a question of getting down the outline, the scaffolding of the story. Then on subsequent revisions I'll see to the rest of it.

Robert Crichton

One thing I learned. It's a working procedure which, I've since heard, was also followed by Hemingway. I call it across the river and into the prose, a method of making it easier to get started when you begin a day's writing.

During World War II, a friend of mine served in the Alaska Scouts which had squads of American soldiers and a few detachments of Indians. He told me that when the American squads would come to a river at the end of a day's march, they would wade across and build fires and dry their clothing before bedding down for the night. The Indians would do just the opposite—bed down on the near shore of the river and start in the morning, fording the stream and getting soaking wet.

When the Americans started to march next morning, dry and comfortable, they advanced cautiously and slowly to keep dry.

There's nothing harder than trying to start on something brand-new when you come to work in the morning. Leave some of what you were doing the night before unfinished so that you can start the next day on familiar ground, or in a familiar river getting your feet wet, and moving on from there easily. The Indians, soaking wet from crossing the river, wouldn't bother about being cautious.

I used the Indian approach to starting a day of writing. The night before I would quit work before crossing the river ahead. I would stop with a paragraph or a page unfinished, knowing what I was going to write in the next few sentences but deliberately leaving them for the morning.

Annie Dillard

The reason to perfect a piece of prose as it progresses—to secure each sentence before building on it—is that original writing fashions a form. It unrolls out into nothingness. It grows cell to cell, bole to bough to twig to leaf; any careful word may suggest a root, may begin a strand of metaphor or event out of which much, or all, will develop.

Leon Edel

I try to write without consulting my material; this avoids interruption and prevents me from overloading my text with quotations. In this way, I establish a comfortable distance from the mass and pressure of data. It helps the narrative flow; it is a guard against irrelevancies.

William Faulkner

There are some kinds of writing that you have to do very fast, like riding a bicycle on a tightrope.

F. Scott Fitzgerald

All good writing is *swimming under water* and holding your breath.

André Gide

Too often I wait for the sentence to finish taking shape in my mind before setting it down. It is better to seize it by the end that first offers itself, head and foot, though not knowing the rest, then pull: the rest will follow along.

Ernest Hemingway

The best way is always to stop when you are going good and when you know what will happen next. If you do that every day when you're rewriting a novel you will never be stuck.

Tony Hillerman

The First Chapter Law is, "Don't spend much time on it. You're going to have to rewrite it." It has proved true for me and I suspect it is true for all of us poor souls who can't draw a blueprint and have to let our stories grow as they go.

Francois Mauriac

When I cease to be carried along, when I no longer feel as though I were taking down dictation I stop.

V. S. Naipaul

The speed of the narrative—that was the speed of the writer. And everything that was later to look like considered literary devices came only from the anxiety of the writer. I wanted above all to take the story to the end. I feared that if I stopped too long anywhere I might lose faith in what I was doing, give up once more, and be left with nothing. And I was conscious, with Gordon Wooford's help, of certain things I had stumbled on the previous day: never to let the words get too much in the way, to be fast, to add one concrete detail to another, and above all to keep the tone tight.

Joyce Carol Oates

I usually write very quickly, chapter by chapter, though I try to alternate work on a novel with shorter pieces—stories, articles, or reviews—in order to keep some objectivity.

Frank O'Connor

"Get black on white" used to be Maupassant's advice . . . ; that's what I always do. I don't give a hoot what the writing's like, I write any sort of rubbish which will cover the main outlines of the story; then I can begin to see it.

Harold Pinter

I follow what I see on the paper in front of me—one sentence after another.

Roger Rosenblatt

Each paragraph almost discovers the paragraph it precedes. When I end one paragraph I know it must lead to another.

Robert Stone

One is improvising when one writes, and you pick up in the same way a musician starts to improvise and detect the inner structure of what he's playing—that's the way I think it works in the writing of a novel. You pick up the beat.

Tom Stoppard

. . . writing is largely a matter of catching things in mid-flight as they flash by, rather than assembling given components and fiddling about with them on a paper until they look pretty.

Henry David Thoreau

Write while the heat is in you. When the farmer burns a hole in his yoke, he carries the hot iron quickly from the fire to the wood, for every moment it is less effectual to penetrate it. It must be used instantly, or it is useless. The writer who postpones the recording of his thoughts uses an iron which has cooled. . . .

Hugo von Hofmannsthal

This thread I spin out of my body and at the same time the thread serves as my path through the air.

Elizabeth Yates

Write. Write in the full flow of the inspiration that has taken hold of you. Don't stop to find the exact word or to correct the construction of a sentence; don't worry yourself over a point of grammar. If in need of a word, leave a space, and when you read your work back to yourself later on you may find that the word comes to you then; but if it doesn't, you can take all the time you need to seek it out. The intensity that is yours when you first begin to write may not last too long, so use it. . . .

other quotations that help me write:

other quotations that help me write:

12

recognizing form

Sometimes I outline what I am going to write or have an outline in my head; other times—almost always in fiction and always in poetry—I feel my way along in the dark. But in every case I am trying *not* to impose a previously constructed form on the text but rather trying to reveal the organic form of the text.

By organic form I mean the shape and structure that grows out of the meaning. It may be a traditional form or the combination of several traditional forms, but the writer has to have the illusion that he or she is discovering the form for the first time, not using something left over from a previous writing or another writer.

You can make a mysterious and complicated matter out of the concept of organic form if you wish, but it's really quite simple. Everything in the piece should relate to each other in a way that leads the reader through the piece to a dominant meaning. And the genre and shape of the piece should be appropriate to that meaning and how it is developed.

For years I have kept playing with the quotation from Hokusai, "If you want to draw a bird, you must become a bird." I am fascinated with drawing and, obviously, I see a relationship between the discoveries I make while drawing the line and writing the line.

I look back in my daybook and see "my ~~pen~~brush draws the iris and it is not the blossom seen but drawn. Line shows the eye what was not in vision. . . ." Prosy, bad writing, but a scratch that I was itching. Four days later:

You see that tree. I become that tree.
It is not easy to enter into things.
squirrels
birds
dropping of leaves

147

grugprs [can't read scribble] bark
forcing roots down

There is, for me, in that scribbled list, a hint of an organic form, a shape that may lead to meaning and contain meaning, a sort of sculpture of language. Later that day, or the next day, I used words to fill out and reveal the form, quickly drafting, then shaping. I looked at the poem, not outside the poem, to see its internal relationships. Here it is:

Until the First Line Leads

When drawing I became the tree,
suffered the bother of birds,
the sadness of leaves, drifting
to earth, the strain of roots,
searching in darkness. A house,
I could not get used to shutting out,
closing in, the strain of secrets.
I never understood the responsibility
of roofing, felt the sudden heat rising
inside the chimney. I was that rock
over there, discovered it mourned
the slow separation from ledge.
My first person, a silent old man
echoed with the roar of memories.
It was not play when the girl lived
hide and seek. One night I entered
the body of a young man dying, felt
the letting go. I fear my pen,
black ink, white paper, but am stranger
to myself until the first line leads.

I could break that form apart, use four-line stanzas or three, make the lines longer or shorter, turn it into a paragraph, make it a prose poem, make it prose, make it an essay. But, for me, the internal order or structure and the external shape or form both contain and reveal the meaning.

Reading it over, I like the title, which came from the last line and was added after the poem told me what it meant. I like taking the time with the tree so the reader has the experience. This allows me to speed up the poem later and describe the other experiences more briefly. I was surprised by the "bother of birds," something that I only felt when I became a tree. I also liked the action of roots. I saw houses differently becoming a house, found out how rocks felt about the ledge. In writing the poem I discovered again my terror of writing and my terrible need to write. And each point seemed to lead to the next. I worry a bit that if I had written a better poem, I would not have to have the last lines. But I didn't write that poem, I wrote this one. I'll send it off.

Try this yourself. Pursue an image in writing. Look for those connections it makes, that shape that it assumes, and you'll begin to understand organic form, that form that is not imposed from without like martial law, but arises from within.

Edward Albee
The problem is finding the correct organic shape and the emotional shape for a piece. The choice of words is a secondary matter.

Robert Anderson
I always tell students in my writing classes that the material chooses its own form.

W. H. Auden
I always have two things in my head—I always have a theme and the form. The form looks for the theme, theme looks for the form, and when they come together you're able to write.

Elizabeth Bowen
Plot might seem to be a matter of choice. It is not. The particular plot for the particular novel is something the novelist is driven to. It is what is left after the whittling-away of alternatives. The novelist is confronted . . . by the impossibility of saying what is to be said in any other way.

Joyce Cary
Your form is your meaning, and your meaning dictates the form.

Anton Chekhov
If in the first chapter you say that a gun hung on the wall, in the second or third chapter it must without fail be discharged.

George M. Cohan
In Act 1, get your characters up a tree; in Act 2, throw stones at them; and in Act 3, get them down again.

I. Compton-Burnett
A plot is like the bones of a person, not interesting like expression or signs of experience, but the support of the whole.

Evan S. Connell, Jr.

There are times a story exceeds the bounds you planned for it and seems to be exceeding those bounds in an organic way. That's one of the things you hope for.

Robert Coover

Stories tend to appear to me, not as formal ideas, but as metaphors seem to demand structures of their own: they seem to have an internal need for a certain form. They're the germ, the thought, the image, the idea, out of which all the rest grows. They're always a bit elusive, involving thoughts, feelings, abstractions, visual material, all at once. I suppose they're a little like dream fragments, in that such fragments always contain, if you analyze them, so much more than at first you suspect.

Robert Cormier

I keep thinking of my rubber-band theory. You have a rubber band that you keep pulling and pulling and pulling, and just at the moment of snapping you release it and start another chapter and start pulling again.

When I write, I never think of segments as chapters; I think of them as scenes. I always visualize them in my mind. Then I try to get the scene down on paper as closely as I can.

Norman Cousins

The writer makes his living by anecdotes. He searches them out and craves them as the raw materials of his profession. No hunter stalking his prey is more alert to the presence of his quarry than a writer looking for small incidents that cast a strong light on human behavior . . . very little has meaning to the writer except as it is tied to the reality of a single person, and except as that reality can illustrate a larger lesson or principle.

Robert Creeley

Elsewhere I remember I did say that "Form is never more than an extension of content," and by that I meant that the thing to be said, will, in that way, determine how it will be said.

Joan Didion

I don't have an outline or a logical sense of where to begin. I just start and hope things will fall into place. It kind of emerges as you go along. Maybe about a third of the way through I will begin to develop some general idea, probably nothing more specific than, say, three parts. Even this is open to change. This kind of inchoate groping seems to be the only way I can approach the thing.

E. L. Doctorow

Stories were as important to survival as a spear or a hoe. They were the memory of the knowledge of the dead. They gave counsel. They connected the visible to the invisible. They distributed the suffering so that it could be borne.

Nell Dunn

There must be a sense of a journey *into* characters. And they must be deeply affected by one another.

Leslie Epstein

One line of dialogue is worth paragraphs of description. No matter what you say about a character, if he doesn't *speak*, he hasn't truly come alive.

Gustave Flaubert

Has a drinking song ever been written by a drunken man? It is wrong to think that feeling is everything. In the arts, it is nothing without form.

Ken Follett

I used to think that in mysteries or thrillers the action and intrigue were important and not the characters. The truth is that the action and intrigue don't count for anything unless the reader cares about and likes the characters. So in a suspense novel, the most important thing—the first consideration—is that the characterization has to be good.

Ford Maddox Ford

Before everything a story must convey a sense of inevitability: that which happens in it must seem to be the only thing that could have happened. . . . The problem of the author is to make his (their) action the only action that character could have taken.

Robert Frost

There is at least so much good in the world that it admits of form and the making of form. And not only admits of it, but calls for it. . . . The background is hugeness and confusion shading away from where we stand into black and utter chaos; and against the background any small manmade figure of order and concentration. . . . To me any little form I assert upon it is . . . to be considered for how much more it is than nothing.

William Gibson

A play begins when a world in some state of equipoise, always uneasy, is broken into by a happening. Since it is not equipoise we have paid to see, but the loosing and binding of an evening's disorder, the sooner the happening the better. . . .

Ernest Hemingway

Prose is architecture not interior decoration.

Henrik Ibsen

As a rule, I make three drafts of my dramas which differ very much from each other in characterization, not in action. When I proceed to the first sketch of the material I feel as though I had the degree of acquaintance with my characters that one acquires on a railway journey; one has met and chatted about this or that. With the next draft I see everything more clearly, I know the characters just about as one would know them after a few weeks' stay in a spa; I have learned the fundamental traits in their characters as well as their little peculiarities; yet it is not impossible that I might make an error in some essential matter. In the last draft, finally, I stand at the limit of knowledge; I know my people from close and long association—they are my intimate friends, who will not disappoint me in any way; in the manner in which I see them now, I shall always see them.

John Irving

A novel is a piece of architecture. It's not random wallowings or confessional diaries. It's a building—it has to have walls and floors and the bathrooms have to work.

Garrison Keillor

Every story finds its *own* form. Finding that form is the great struggle of writing, for which there is no prescription.

Arthur Koestler

In the true novel, as opposed to reportage and chronicle, the main action takes place inside the characters' skulls and ribs.

Arthur Kopit

I had three or four bulletin boards in my office. I started pinning up the cards, and then shifting them around, looking for a sequence. Eventually, the play found its shape.

Denise Levertov

Form is never more than a revelation of content.

C. S. Lewis

I sometimes think that writing is like driving sheep down a road. If there is any gate to the left or right, the readers will most certainly go into it.

Gabriel García Márquez

The image grows in my head until the whole story takes shape as it might in real life. The problem is that life isn't the same as literature, so then I have to ask myself the big question: How do I adapt this, what is the most appropriate structure for the book? I have always aspired to finding the perfect structure. One perfect structure in literature is that of Sophocles' *Oedipus Rex*. Another is a short story, "Monkey's Paw," by an English writer, William Jacobs.

Vincent McHugh

From first to last, the novelist is concerned with character. In the novel, everything is character, just as everything is tone or process. Each event must be focused in a human consciousness. Without someone to look at it, there is no landscape; no idea without someone to conceive it, and no passion without persons.

*

Always the specific in a novel: the scene *seen*, the word *heard*, the deed *done*.

Arthur Miller

I wanted a play [*Death of a Salesman*], that is, that had almost a biological life of its own. It would be as incontrovertible as the musculature of the human body. Everything connecting with everything else, all of it working according to plan. No excesses. Nothing explaining itself; all of it simply inevitable, as one structure, as one corpus. We have to remember that, maybe more than any other art, the play lacks independence as an artifact. It is a set of relationships. There really are no characters in plays; there are *relationships*. Where there are only characters and no relationships, we have an unsatisfactory play.

Marsha Norman

I'm convinced that there are absolutely unbreakable rules in the theater, and that it doesn't matter how good you are, you can't break them. . . . You must state the issue at the beginning of the play. The audience must know what is at stake; they must know when they will be able to go home: "This is a story of a little boy who lost his marbles." They must know, when the little boy either gets his marbles back or finds something that is better than his marbles, or kills himself because he can't live without his marbles, that the play will end and they can applaud and go home. He can't *not* care about the marbles. He has to want them with such a passion that you are interested, that you connect to that passion. The theater is all about wanting things that you can or can't have or you do or do not get. Now, the boy himself has to be likable. It has to matter to you whether he gets his marbles or not. The other things—language, structure, et cetera—are variables. One other thing: You can't stop the action for detours. On the way to finding his marbles, the boy can't stop and go swimming. He might do that in a novel, but not in a play.

Joyce Carol Oates

Strange people appear in my thoughts and define themselves slowly to me: first their faces, then their personalities and quirks and personal histories, then their relationships with other people, who very slowly appear, and a kind of "plot" then becomes clear to me as I figure out how all these people came together and what they are doing. I can see them at times very closely, and indeed I "am" them—my personality merges with theirs. At other times I can see them from a distance; the general shape of their lives, which will be transformed into a novel, becomes clear to me; so I try to put this all together, working very slowly; never hurrying the process. I can't hurry it any more than I can prevent it.

Flannery O'Connor

The more you write, the more you will realize that the form is organic, that it is something that grows out of the material, that the form of each story is unique. . . .

Charles Olson

Form is never more than an extension of content.

Robert B. Parker

The plot is the line on which I hang the wash, and the wash is what I care about.

John Sayles

I try to envision the story as a silent movie before I start adding dialogue.

Neil Simon

Dialogue surprises me. Dialogue comes last. I think of characters first.

Isaac Bashevis Singer

When you write a novel or a novella, make each chapter tell a new development of the story and contain as much information as the first one. It must be revealing, rich in images, in character description, small in quantity and long in quality.

Ivan Turgenev

I never started from ideas but always from character.

Mark Twain

Don't say the old lady screamed—bring her on and let her scream.

Anne Tyler

Mostly, it's lies, writing novels. You set out to tell an untrue story and you try to make it believable, even to yourself. Which calls for details; any good lie does. I'm quicker to believe I was once a circus aerialist if I remember that just before every performance, I used to dip my hands in a box of chalk powder that smelled like clean, dry cloth being torn.

Maybe, in fact, I once was a circus aerialist. One lie leads to another; the tangled web you weave gives birth to events on its own. But that's if things are going well. I can tell they're going well when the words start running ahead of themselves.

Kurt Vonnegut, Jr.

Don't put anything in a story that does not reveal character or advance the action.

Chad Walsh

The form of the poem should seem, when the poem is finished, as inevitable—and invisible—as a man's skeleton.

Eudora Welty

All fiction writers work by indirection; to show, not to tell; not to make statements about a character, but to demonstrate it in his actions or his conversations or by suggesting his thoughts, so that the reader understands for himself. Because fiction accomplishes its ends by using the oblique.

*

Dialogue has to show not only something about the speaker that is its own revelation, but also maybe something about the speaker that he doesn't know but the other character does know. You've got to show a two-way revelation between speaker and listener, which is the fascination of writing dialogue. Dialogue is action.

Richard Wilbur

Form comes about for me in a perfectly natural way. I have never said to myself "now I'll write a sonnet." I write a few lines that interest me and discover they become a sonnet.

other quotations that help me write:

other quotations that help me write:

other quotations that help me write:

13

at play with language

Now we observe the writer at play, using the materials of our trade to say what the writer hasn't said before in a way the writer—and reader—hasn't heard before.

The writer has great respect for language. The writer sees what can be made out of words left in and words left out; connects words that slide easily together or ignites the civil war of the phrase; allows sentences to run free or scrambles after them to bring them up short; inserts or extracts commas, periods, colons, and semicolons, even dashes; breaks lines and mends others; constructs paragraphs that slow the reader down and propel the reader through the text; seeks *the word* that sounds right and is right.

The love affair with language is not always easy. The writer is a demanding lover, always asking more of language. But there is joy and excitement in this relationship as change brings more change. As more is revealed, language will never be quite the same because of the revealing.

Each day the writer returns to word play—clause play, sentence play, paragraph play—constantly surprised that this old lover is forever young, forever the provider of surprise, delight, and insight.

Marvin Bell
  I did teach myself to write mostly by abandoning myself to the language, seeing what it wanted to say to me.

Heinrich Böll

Behind every word a whole world is hidden that must be imagined. Actually, every word has a great burden of memories, not only just of one person but of all mankind. Take a word such as bread, or war; take a word such as chair, or bed or Heaven. Behind every word is a whole world.

Don DeLillo

Working at sentences and rhythms is probably the most satisfying thing I do as a writer. I think after a while a writer can begin to know himself through his language. He sees someone or something reflected back at him from these constructions. Over the years it's possible for a writer to shape himself as a human being through the language he uses. I think written language, fiction, goes that deep. He not only sees himself but begins to make himself or remake himself.

Joan Didion

What I know about grammar is its infinite power. To shift the structure of a sentence alters the meaning of that sentence, as definitely and inflexibly as the position of a camera alters the meaning of the object photographed. Many people know about camera angles now, but not so many know about sentences.

Gustave Flaubert

Whatever the thing you wish to say, there is but one word to express it, but one verb to give it movement, but one adjective to qualify it; you must seek until you find this noun, this verb, this adjective.

Richard Ford

Just to write a good sentence—that's the postulate I go by. I guess I've always felt that if you could keep a kind of fidelity toward the individual sentence, that you could work toward the rest.

Theodor Geisel [Dr. Seuss]

Writing simply means no dependent clauses, no dangling things, no flashbacks, and keeping the subject near the predicate. We throw in as many fresh words as we can get away with. Simple, short sentences don't always work. You have to do tricks with pacing, alternate long sentences with short, to keep it vital and alive. Virtually every page is a cliffhanger—you've got to force them to turn it.

Graham Greene

There are, of course, basic principles to be observed: Adjectives are to be avoided unless they are strictly necessary; adverbs too, which is even more important. When I open a book and find that so and so has "answered sharply" or "spoken tenderly," I shut it again: It's the dialogue itself which should express the sharpness or the tenderness without any need to use adverbs to underline them.

John Hersey

The reward of writing is in the writing itself. It comes with finding the right word. The quest for a superb sentence is a groping for honesty, a search for the innermost self, a self-discipline, a generous giving out of one's most intimate rhythms and meanings.

James Joyce

I have the words already. What I am seeking is the perfect order of words in the sentence. You can see for yourself how many different ways they might be arranged.

Jerzy Kosinski

The idea is always to remove the language as much as possible so the language will not attract attention.

Denise Levertov

I believe every space and comma is a living part of the poem and has its function, just as every muscle and pore of the body has its function. And the way the lines are broken is a functioning part essential to the life of the poem.

William Meredith

It starts with an insight which gets a few words close to the ground and then the words begin to make specific the insight. Once they start growing the words are seminal—I suppose it's like the bacteria of a growth. I can hardly remember a poem in which the words are not *particular* words, often very bleak, simple words. Once they are put down they are able to focus an idea.

George Moore

Anyone who can improve a sentence of mine by the omission or placing of a comma is looked upon as my dearest friend.

Marianne Moore

Words cluster like chromosomes, determining procedure.

*

Poetry is all nouns and verbs.

Samuel Eliot Morison

Use direct rather than indirect statements, the active rather than the passive voice, and make every sentence and paragraph an organic whole.

Toni Morrison

The language must be careful and must appear effortless. It must not sweat. It must suggest and be provocative at the same time. It is the thing that black people love so much—the saying of words, holding them on the tongue, experimenting with them, playing with them.

George Orwell

(i) Never use a metaphor, simile or other figure of speech which you are used to seeing in print.

(ii) Never use a long word where a short one will do.

(iii) If it is possible to cut a word out, always cut it out.

(iv) Never use the passive where you can use the active.

(v) Never use a foreign phrase, a scentific word or jargon word if you can think of an everday English equivalent.

(vi) Break any of these rules sooner than say anything barbarous.

Theodore Roethke

I am overwhelmed by the beautiful disorder of poetry, the eternal virginity of words.

Charles Simic

The only principle of technique I'm aware of is faith. Faith to the language and faith to the situation to which that language points. Nothing else. . . .

William Stafford

When I write, grammar is my enemy; the materials of my craft come at me in a succession of emergencies in which my feelings are ambivalent; I do not have any commitments, just opportunities.

*

I'm not alone when I'm writing—the language itself, like a kind of trampoline, is there helping me.

Barbara Tuchman

I try for motion in every paragraph. I hate sentences that begin, "There was a storm." Instead, write, "A storm burst."

Mark Twain

The difference between the right word and the almost-right word is the difference between lightning and a lightning-bug.

Voltaire

The adjective is the enemy of the noun.

E. B. White

English usage is something more than mere taste, judgement, and education—sometimes it's sheer luck, like getting across a street.

other quotations that help me write:

other quotations that help me write:

_____

14

the closing line

I used to think I never knew the end before I began and then, in rereading my daybooks, I saw scenes, anecdotes, quotations, facts, revealing specifics that were marked with a "k" for kicker. I had noted what might make an effective ending.

I do not, however, write the end first as many writers do. I can see why they do it—knowing the ending gives the writer a sense of destination.

The danger for me would be that I might drive the text toward that end, despite the fact that the text might be moving toward another, more appropriate, conclusion. Still, we must pay attention to those writers who do write the end first and play with this possibility ourselves to see if it helps. And even if I don't do it all of the time, it may be a necessary solution on a particular writing project.

Try an experiment. In writing a scene or chapter in a novel, I will put at the bottom of my daybook page an action I expect to happen:

she walks out of his hospital room

Then I walk through the scene, watching to see what actions will lead to that action:

police come to door
father has been shot
rushes to hospital
asks for father
nurse says, "You mean suicide" attempt
rushes to room
Trixie with him, both high, both laughing
She walks

Now write it quickly. Notice how the sense of destination influences the writing. But, of course, allow the scene to take its own course. I may discover she does not walk.

This may not be "the" way I write—in fact I rarely write this way. But when I do, it solves a problem I haven't been able to solve any other way.

Truman Capote

I always write the end of everything first. I always write the last chapters of my books before I write the beginning. I wrote the end of "Answered Prayers" seven or eight years ago. It runs about 300 pages. Then I go back to the beginning. I mean, it's always nice to know where you're going, is my theory.

Raymond Carver

Most often I know how a story is going to end early on. I get the first line and the ending some way ahead.

Richard Condon

There's nothing mind-boggling about creating a story. I developed a set of characters and decided in advance how they'd end up in the story, their fate. I worked backwards. I always work backwards. Everything the characters do, how they react, where they go, what happens to them—is all focused and channeled to how they end up. I know the characters' destination in the narrative sense before I even start to write.

John Gregory Dunne

It is a peculiarity of mine that I always know the last sentence of a book before I begin.

William Gibson

I always know the end. The end of everything I write is somehow always implicit from the beginning. What I don't know is the middle. I don't know how I'm going to get there.

Joseph Heller

I know when I'm done because I usually have the last paragraph of the last chapter written before I start writing the second chapter.

Raymond Hill

The last words I write of a book are very often the first, so it doesn't much matter how you start.

S. E. Hinton

My characters always take shape first; they wander around my mind looking for something to do. I know I'm ready to put them in a story when an ending comes to mind. The ending always comes first.

Christopher Lafarge

I have never yet begun to write a short story or a novel when I did not see in advance, with a clarity that occasionally found its expression in the actual words, the ending of that story.

Tom Lea

When I started *The Brave Bulls*, I knew the first line, and before I could go on I had to know the last line.

John McPhee

I always know the last line of a story before I've written the first one. Going through all that creates the form and the shape of the thing. It also relieves the writer, once you know the structure, to concentrate each day on one thing. You know right where it fits.

Toni Morrison

I always know the ending; that's where I start. I don't always have a beginning, so I don't always know how to start a book.

Joyce Carol Oates

I always know exactly how the novel will end, even the wording of the final paragraph.

Cynthia Ozick

If you're writing a story and confused about the end, go back to the first sentence.

Katherine Anne Porter

There are a hundred ways to begin a story but only one to end it, and the writer must know the end before he begins.

Roger Rosenblatt

Sometimes I organize a piece so carefully that I will not only know the general thought I want to end with, I will write the last sentence before having written anything else. This sentence will contain all of the feeling of a piece unwritten, but I know it will be there and almost always I'm right.

Robert Stone

I know the beginning and usually the end. My problem is the middle— the second act, so to speak.

Eudora Welty

I think the end is implicit in the beginning. It must be. If that isn't there in the beginning, you don't know what you're working toward. You should have a sense of a story's shape and form and its destination, all of which is like a flower inside a seed.

other quotations that help me write:

other quotations that help me write:

other quotations that help me write: _____

15

*the pleasures
of revision*

Unlike our students, most of us do not see revising and editing as punishment. We see it as opportunity. We have been building castles out of air; now there is a tangible object, and we can go to work to make it work.

We revel in the craft of making the larger changes in a text—revising—and at the precise, line-by-line, word-by-word refining of the text—editing. Here our skills have a clear task: make it true, make it clear, make it graceful.

I enjoy cutting, reordering, developing, shaping, polishing my drafts. Never have I failed to make a text better by my revising and editing. I cannot say that has always been true when others have revised and edited my texts, but it is true when I have practiced surgery on my own words.

There are few things more satisfying than this form of participatory reading, where the acts of reading and writing incite new reading, new writing, line by line.

Nonwriters think of revision as a matter of tinkering, touching up, making presentable, but writers know it is central to the act of discovering. Allow me to take you within the game of revision. I am going to work on what may become a poem, right now, in front of you, to reveal my own pleasures in revision—and to demonstrate the importance of writing badly to write well. I will not purposely write badly. I don't have to. I'll just let the writing come however it will.

I look through my daybook. No lines I want to follow. Abandoned lines, abandoned drafts, better left where they are. Mozart plays on the hi-fi, I try to put out of my mind last night's phone call, this morning's phone call, the problem my wife is having with our financial records, the phone call from an editor I expect any moment, the letters I should write, and allow myself to become empty, receptive, quiet.

I make a cup of tea, crunch a cracker, remember the mood of the counsel of the writers in this book, allow myself to move backward in reverie. The

171

writing will be private. You will not understand its meaning. No matter. I do not either.

    reading silence
    going in other rooms
    father so nattily dressed
    uniforms
    boots
    lonely for the relatives I never had
    never so lonely as at family gatherings

Perhaps I Was Adopted

I ~~slid~~ slide under the Thanksgiving table,
~~studied~~ study the shadow~~ing~~ world of knees,
smells ~~and~~ the myster~~ies~~y of women.
~~Not even in this cave was quiet.~~
The uncle who never smiled, roared.
~~with what might have been laughter.~~
Men barked ~~and~~ snorted ~~and~~ bellowed,
women giggled ~~and~~ gasped, bent to whisper
to each other. ~~and h~~His hairy hand danced

Phone call from the editor. We work on a piece of nonfiction ready to go to the printer. Problems with connecting by phone, other phone calls, I doodle with the poem above, crossing out, making it more active. I'll copy it over probably cutting out the line about the uncle who never smiled and start playing with this again after lunch. Something worth pursuing here? I dunno. I won't find out if I don't fool around some more. I pasted the draft above in my daybook and left for lunch.

On the walk to the Bagelry I kept "writing" the poem in my head. I got there early, sat at the farthest back table and revised. First we have to put in, then we may take out—or move around. I began by editing the copy in the daybook.

~~Perhaps I Was Adopted~~

~~Now, when the party is loud I return~~

I ~~slid~~ slide under the Thanksgiving table,
~~studied~~ study the shadow~~ing~~ world of knees,
smells ~~and~~ the myster~~ies~~y of women.
~~Not even in this cave was quiet.~~
The uncle who never smiled, roared.
~~with what might have been laughter.~~
~~Men barked and snorted and bellowed,~~

~~women giggled and gasped, bent to whisper~~
~~to each other. and~~ hHis hairy hand danced

on ~~Mother's~~ knee
   sister's

Family Secrets

We kept the shades drawn, never released
laughter through open windows, fought
with silence but on Thanksgiving I slid
under the dining room table, studied the underside
of leaves that stretched it out for relatives,
studied the shadowy world of knees, smelled [smelt]
the mystery of women. Heard the uncle who never laughed,
never married, roar at Father's story, ~~saw~~ watched
his hairy hand dance on sister's knee.
~~Today I have escaped~~
I am alien from such festivities, do not wear
the mask of hearty laughter, even avoid
the comradeship of funerals but wonder
what my daughters ~~whisper~~ know of family,
what they overheard, how these spies

inform

Then I wrote an insert for the space above "I am alien":

I saw mother sneak the medicine bottle, heard father
betray her on the telephone, learned my own disloyalities.

This was not autobiography, I have no sister, but there is something here
that I may return to. But now, back at my desk, I am haunted (pun intended)
by "the comradeship of funerals."

At the family plot we gather ~~to~~ for release
~~another~~ from a life of born in sin, ~~of never~~
~~being good enough.~~ Strangers we stand alone,
collars turned up against the rain, heads
bowed as if in prayer. ~~Only at funerals~~
~~we meet to confront what we were, what might~~
~~have been.~~ Under the Thanksgiving table
I watched his hairy hand dance on sister's
knee. (We do not bury family secrets????)

This is the raw material, the awful stuff we do not reveal, but, embarrassed
and ashamed, I show you what I did in this experiment. My cutting, tossing

away, exposing, extending, drawing back, moving around, doing over, rereading, rewriting will go in my daybook. Perhaps I will continue to draft and revise. Perhaps not, but this reveals one writer at work—and at play.

There is a danger, however, in the seductive craft of revision. Many times I no longer do much revision. There is no virtue in publishing what comes easily or with struggle; no pride should be wasted on "That's a first draft," or "I did eighty-three rewrites of those twelve lines." Each text has its own demand and we must accept the deadline and allow our texts to go as we must allow our children to leave home, knowing they are not yet perfect but ready to enter the world.

It is the text that controls. I thought that poem was dead and told myself I would include it unfinished in this book. A day or two later, however, I was sitting in a parking lot while my wife shopped for dinner and I found myself writing.

> I am still hidden under the dining room table
> in the kingdom of knees listen[ing to] ~~the~~ stories
> I ~~cannot understand, hearing the strange music~~
> ~~of laughter, (family acting as if)~~
>
> ~~smell of lamb~~
>
>   will never understand. Worried
> by the wild jiggling foot. At his funeral
> I heard his nervous, tapping, tapping.

I was fascinated by that tapping foot, but my wife rolled out the groceries, we loaded them in the car and drove off. Then a morning, several days later, I turned to the poem again. All I knew was that the hand on the knee was too much and not honest. What really went on was more terrifying than that. Quickly I wrote the following, purposely *not* looking back at what I had written before. I might check that later—now all I wanted to work with was what was written in my head.

Thanksgiving

> At Thanksgiving dinner I slid under the table,
> hoping for silence. I had learned to read the unsaid,
> decode the turning away, the hesitant reaching out, the quick
> withdrawal. I was comfortable with loneliness and now
> the uncles came, their voices unnatural, loud, hearty
> as if they were not deacons. They told the stories
> they always told, barking at the familiar lines, grinning
> at the women gasped, competing for seconds, thirds,
> playing family and I sat cross legged under the table,
> not missed, studying the kingdom of knees, inhaling

the mystery of women, waiting for their going
and the return of our separartness, how motherleaves the room
when Dad comes, how father wanders a stranger in our flat,
how I can pass through the pages of a book, read by flashlight
under the covers. In the wars of silence, I go to ground.
Delivering the paper I am scholar of lighted windows,
researcher of families that remain in the same room,
sometimes in summer I hear laughter, the exciting cry
of hate, of fear. How I envied the butcher's daughter
whose father, Emil, chased her mother around the block,
how the light glinted off his shining blade.

Then I typed in the poem on my computer, reading and revising.

Thanksgiving

I slid under the table (At Thanksgiving dinner),
~~hoping for~~ seeking silence. I ~~had learned to~~ could read the
unsaid,
decode the ~~(quick)~~ turning away, the hesitant reaching out, ~~the~~
quick withdrawal (but not the roar of family). ~~I was~~
~~e~~Comfortable
with loneliness ~~and now~~ the uncles, ~~came,~~ wived or alone,
the stranger cousins, ~~their voices unnatural, loud, hearty~~
~~as if they were not~~ hearty voices, jolly, unnatural in
deacons.
~~They~~ Father told the stories ~~they~~ he always told, (they bellowed)
~~barking~~ at the familiar lines, grinning
~~at~~ as the women gasped. (The men) compet~~ing~~ed for seconds,
thirds,
play~~ing~~ed family and I ~~sat~~ hid cross legged under the table,
~~not missed,~~ studying the kingdom of knees, inhaling
the mystery of women,
waiting for the~~ir~~ (bustle of) their going, ~~and~~ the return
~~of our~~ (to) separartness, how mother leaves the room when Dad
comes, how father wanders a stranger in our flat, (flees to the
street)
~~how I can pass through the pages of a book, read by flashlight~~
~~under the covers.~~ In the wars of silence, I go to ground.
Delivering the paper
I ~~am~~ become scholar ~~of~~ to lighted windows, ~~researcher~~ collector
of families that remain in the same room, sometimes in summer
I hear laughter, the ~~exciting~~ thrilling cry of hate, of fear.
How I envied the butcher's daughter whose father, Emil, chased
her mother around the block, ~~how~~ the light glint~~ed~~ing ~~of~~ from his
shining blade.

Now I type this version up, making more changes, all aimed at releasing the poem from the page, allowing it to reconstruct feelings I didn't know I had, feelings that might be released in some readers if they read this poem. They would not have my experience, my feelings, but the poem would cause each reader to have individual experiences and feelings made articulate by my private explorations gone public.

Revision—look at that word: re-seeing—is a simple matter of putting in, taking out, reordering until the written line drawn, erased and redrawn, allows you to see what you are writing and what it means.

In the Kingdom of Knees

I slid under the table at Sunday dinner,
seeking silence. I could read the unsaid,
decode turning away, the hesitant reaching out,
quick withdrawal. I was comfortable with loneliness
but feared the roar of uncles, wived or alone, stranger
cousins, jolly voices, unnatural in deacons. Father
told his stories and they bellowed at the familiar pause,
nudging each other as the women gasped. The men competed
for the legs, the women for the wings and I hid cross legged
under the table, studying the kingdom of knees, inhaling
the mystery of women. Even here I knew when the dribble glass
leaked, the hinged spoon spilled sugar, watched Uncle Ben sneak
the whoopee cushion onto mothers chair, watched his knees squeeze
the bladder that made the new wife's plate rise and fall, heard
them waiting for her discomfort, the cruel burst of laughter when
she did. I hid until the bustle of family leaving, the return of
separarteness, how mother leaves the room when Dad comes in, how
father wanders a stranger in our flat, flees to the street. In
their wars of silence, I go to ground. And yet delivering the
evening paper, I am scholar of lighted windows, collector of
families that remain in the same room. Sometimes in summer
I hear laughter, the thrilling cry of hate, of fear. How I envy
the butcher's daughter whose father, Emil, runs her mother down
the block, light glinting from his shining blade.

Is the process of revision finished? Probably not. But it is time to show this draft to a few test readers—Minnie Mae, Anne, Hannah, Mekeel, Chip, Don. And then, well who knows? I didn't know I would begin this poem, follow these confusing lines back to that home I fled but never escaped.

I had thought I was done with the poem, but I had to wait in a dentist's office in Boston and I automatically took out my daybook. I had pasted the poem in, and so I couldn't resist reading it and, reading it, I couldn't resist editing it, the fine-tuning end of the revision spectrum—and before I dare show it to a test reader.

In the Kingdom of Knees

I slid under the table at Sunday dinner,
seeking silence. I ~~could~~ have learned to read the unsaid,
decode turning away, the hesitant reaching out,
quick withdrawal. I was comfortable with loneliness
but feared the roar of uncles, wived or alone, stranger
cousins, jolly voices, unnatural in deacons. Father
told his stories and they bellowed at the familiar pause,
nudging each other as the women gasped. The men competed
for ~~the~~ a turkey legs, ~~the~~ women for the a wings ~~and~~ while I hid
cross legged
under the table, studying the kingdom of knees, inhaling
the mystery of women. Even here I knew when the dribble glass
leaked, the hinged spoon spilled sugar, watched Uncle Ben sneak
the whoopee cushion onto mother's chair, watched his knees
squeeze the bladder that made the new wife's plate rise and fall,
heard them waiting for her discomfort, their ~~cruel burst of~~
laughter. ~~when she did.~~
I hid until the bustle of family leaving, the return of
separa~~r~~teness, how mother leaves the room when Dad comes in, how
father wanders a stranger in our flat, flees to the ~~street~~ phone.
In their wars of silence, I go to ground. ~~And yet, d~~Delivering
the evening paper, I ~~am~~ become scholar of lighted windows,
collector of families that remain in the same room. ~~Sometimes~~
in summer ~~I~~ I ~~stand~~ pause by ~~empty~~ open windowshear laughter, the
thrilling cry of hate, of fear. ~~How~~ I envy the butcher's
daughter whose father, Emil, runs her mother down the block,
light glinting from his shining blade.

In typing this up I will play a bit with line breaks, one of the most important
elements in writing poetry.

In the Kingdom of Knees

I slid under the table at Sunday dinner,
seeking silence. I have just learned to read
the unsaid, decode turning away, the hesitant
reaching out, quick withdrawal, grown comfortable
with loneliness but feared the roar of uncles,
wived or alone, stranger cousins, jolly voices
unnatural in deacons. Father told his stories
and they bellowed at the familiar pause, nudging
each other as the women gasped. The men competed
for a turkey leg, women for a wing while I hid
cross legged under the table, studying the kingdom

of knees, inhaling the mystery of women. Even here
I knew when the dribble glass leaked, the hinged
spoon spilled sugar, watched Uncle Ben sneak
the whoopee cushion onto mother's chair, watched
his knees squeeze the bladder that made the new wife's
plate rise and fall, heard their waiting
for her discomfort, their laughter. I hid until
the bustle of family leaving, the return of separateness,
how mother leaves the room when Dad comes in, how father
wanders a stranger in our flat, flees to the phone.
In their wars of silence, I go to ground. Delivering
the evening paper, I become scholar of lighted windows,
collector of families that remain in the same room.
In summer I pause by open windows hear laughter,
the thrilling cry of hate, of fear. I envy
the butcher's daughter whose father, Emil,
runs her mother down the block, light glinting
from his shining blade.

Yes, I changed a few things. Of course. And then I wondered what would
happen if I broke the poem into stanzas. I write a five line version, then a four
line one. This is play, after all.

Four lines:

I Envy the Butcher's Daughter

I slide under the table at Sunday dinner,
seeking silence. I have just learned to read
the unsaid, decode turning away, the hesitant
reaching out, quick withdrawal, grown familiar

with loneliness but fear the roar of uncles,
wived or alone, stranger cousins, jolly voices
unnatural in deacons. Father tells his stories
and they bellow at the familiar pause, nudging

each other as the women gasp. The men compete
for a turkey leg, women for a wing while I hide
cross legged under the table, study the kingdom
of knees, inhale the mystery of women. Even here

I know when the dribble glass leaks, the hinged
spoon spills sugar, watch Uncle Morison sneak
the whoopee cushion onto mother's chair, watch
his knees squeeze the bladder that makes

his new wife's plate rise and fall, hear
their impatient waiting for her discomfort,
their laughter. I hide until family leaves,
return to separateness. Mother leaves the room

when Dad comes in, father flees to the phone.
In their wars of silence, I go to ground. Delivering
the evening paper, I become scholar of lighted windows,
collector of families that remain in the same room.

In summer I pause by open windows hear laughter,
cries of hate, of fear. I envy the butcher's daughter.
Her father, Emil, runs her mother down the block,
light glinting from his shining blade.

I like the four-line version. It seems to pace the experiences better than the solid text. I also move into the more active present tense; cut and sharpen; return to the truth that it was *his* new wife; make "comfortable" the more accurate "familiar"; get rid of "how" and unnecessary words such as "thrilling." And the title had to be changed.

Now, I'll share it with Mekeel McBride, my mentor in poetry, at lunch tomorrow.

First, Mekeel liked the poem and that's important to me. Would I decide *not* to submit a poem she didn't like? No. Have I sent out poems I didn't think were good enough but she thought were? Yes. What happened to them? Some got published.

I respect her reading and learn from it. She didn't like the word "silence" in the second line. She wrote, "Silence? or privacy? You still *hear* alot down there but you're a little safer." In a moment or two the word "exile" came to me and I think that is truer to the poem—and there is a nice tension in "seeking exile"; it is something you don't usually seek but that was exactly what I was seeking.

She thought the third stanza was strong, resisted "for a turkey leg, women for a wing," then grew to like it. I'll look at that again. It's a spot I worried about. Of the next stanza she wrote, "this is a creepy sequence—the adults act like demented children and the child is a sad wise adult." She also praised the next-to-last stanza and the "powerful, eerie ending." She added that she liked the poem without stanza breaks but agrees with my using them "because this a rich poem + the breaks give me time to take it all in."

So I read it carefully, adding "exile" and seeing if anything else needs to be changed. Is it discouraging to do this? Just the opposite—it is exciting. I am at play. I write another version, taking out, putting in, moving around and finally decide: enough.

I Envy the Butcher's Daughter

I slide under the table at Sunday dinner,
seeking exile. I have just learned to read
the unsaid, slow turning away, the hesitant
reaching out, quick withdrawal, grown content

with loneliness but fear the roar of uncles,
wived or alone, stranger cousins, jolly voices
unnatural in deacons. Father tells his stories
and they bellow at the familiar pause, nudging

each other as the women gasp. The men compete
for a turkey leg, women for a wing while I hide
cross legged under the table, study the kingdom
of knees, inhale the mystery of women. Even here

I know when the dribble glass leaks, the hinged
spoon spills sugar, watch Uncle Morison sneak
the whoopee cushion onto mother's chair, watch
his knees squeeze the bladder that makes

his new wife's plate rise and fall, hear them wait
for her discomfort, hear their laughter explode.
I hide until family leaves, separateness returns.
Mother leaves the room when Dad comes in, father

flees to the phone. In their wars of silence,
I go to ground. Delivering the evening paper,
I become scholar of lighted windows, collector
of families that remain in the same room.

In summer I pause by open windows, hear cries
of hate, of fear. I envy the butcher's daughter.
Her father, Emil, runs her mother down the block,
light glinting from his shining blade.

And what about that foot tapping in the coffin? Well, it's still tapping and
someday . . .

Max Apple
I'm rewriting it while I'm writing it. It's changing itself.

Saul Bellow

I'm happy when the revisons are big. I'm not speaking of stylistic revisions, but of revisions in my own understanding.

John Berger

It's a matter of rewriting and rewriting. If I'm writing a story, I may rewrite a page 10, 12 times.

John Berryman

We take it that all young writers overestimate their work. It's impossible not to—I mean if you recognized what shit you were writing, you wouldn't write it.

Truman Capote

I believe more in the scissors than I do in the pencil.

Raymond Carver

I've done as many as twenty or thirty drafts of a story. Never less than ten or twelve drafts. It's instructive, and heartening both, to look at the early drafts of great writers. I'm thinking of the photographs of galleys belonging to Tolstoy, to name one writer who loved to revise. I mean, I don't know if he loved it or not, but he did a great deal of it. He was always revising, right down to the time of page proofs. He went through and rewrote *War and Peace* eight times and was still making corrections in the galleys. Things like this should hearten every writer whose first drafts are dreadful, like mine are.

*

I like to mess around with my stories. I'd rather tinker with a story after writing it, and then tinker some more, changing this, changing that, than have to write the story in the first place. . . . Maybe I revise because it gradually takes me into the heart of what the story is *about*. I keep trying to see if I can find that out.

John Ciardi

. . . the last act of the writing must be to become one's own reader. It is, I suppose, a schizophrenic process. To begin passionately and to end critically, to begin hot and to end cold; and, more important, to try to be passion-hot and critic-cold at the same time.

Robert Cormier

The beautiful part of writing is that you don't have to get it right the first time, unlike, say, a brain surgeon. You can always do it better, find the exact word, the apt phrase, the leaping simile.

Michael Crichton

Books aren't written, they're rewritten. Including your own. It is one of the hardest things to accept, especially after the seventh rewrite hasn't quite done it.

Roald Dahl

By the time I am nearing the end of a story, the first part will have been reread and altered and corrected at least one hundred and fifty times. I am suspicious of both facility and speed. Good writing is essentially rewriting. I am positive of this.

Len Deighton

I write double-spaced to leave plenty of room for the inevitable revisions and I never write on both sides of the paper. I write on a right hand page, leaving the facing page blank for insertions and revisions. Then I leave the following double-page blank.

James Dickey

I have endless drafts, one after another; and I try out 50, 75, or a hundred variations on a single line sometimes. I work on the process of refining low-grade ore. . . . No. I am not inspired.

Joan Didion

My writing is a process of rewriting, of going back and changing and filling in. In the rewriting process you discover what's going on, and you go back and bring it up to that point. Sometimes you'll just push through, indicate a scene or a character, leave a space, then go back later and fill it in.

Annie Dillard

Several delusions weaken the writer's resolve to throw away work. If he has read his pages too often, those pages will have a necessary quality, the ring of the inevitable, like poetry known by heart; they will perfectly answer their own familiar rhythms. He will retain them. He may retain those pages if they possess some virtues, such as power in themselves, though they lack the cardinal virtue, which is pertinence to, and unity with, the book's thrust. Sometimes the writer leaves his early chapters in place from gratitude; he cannot contemplate them or read them without feeling again the blessed relief that exalted him when the words first appeared—relief that he was writing anything at all. That beginning served to get him where he was going after all; surely the reader needs it, too, as groundwork. But no.

E. L. Doctorow

I don't think anything I've written has been done in under six or eight drafts.

Meister Eckhart
Only the hand that erases can write the true thing.

Deborah Eisenberg
For me, most writing consists of siphoning out useless pre-story matter, cutting and cutting and cutting, what seems to be endless rewriting, and what is entailed in all that is patience, and waiting, and false starts, and dead ends, and really, in a way, nerve.

Ralph Waldo Emerson
Cut these words and they would bleed.

Monroe Engel
The great moment in the making of *Fish* occurred a year and a half ago, when I threw away more than a thousand pages. No, it wasn't a painful experience; it was a kind of liberation. You see, I did what I always tell my students not to do. In my impatience to go somewhere, I allowed the book to get ahead of me.

John Fowles
All the best cutting is done when one is sick of the writing.

John Kenneth Galbraith
In my own case there are days when the result is so bad that no fewer than five revisions are required. However, when I'm greatly inspired, only four revisions are needed before, as I've often said, I put in that note of spontaneity which even my meanest critics concede.

William Gass
I work not by writing but by rewriting. Each sentence has many drafts. Eventually there is a paragraph. This gets many drafts. Eventually there is a page. This gets many drafts.

Ellen Goodman
What makes me happy is rewriting. In the first draft you get your ideas and your theme clear, if you are using some kind of metaphor you get that established, and certainly you have to know where you're coming out. But the next time through it's like cleaning house, getting rid of all the junk, getting things in the right order, tightening things up. I like the process of making writing neat.

Graham Greene
I aim to be content with what I produce. It's an aim I never achieve, but I go over my work word by word, time and again, so as to be as little dissatisfied as possible.

Ernest Hemingway

Hemingway: ".... I rewrote the ending to *Farewell to Arms,* the last page of it, thirty-nine times before I was satisfied."
Plimpton: "Was there some technical problem there? What was it that had you stumped?"
Hemingway: "Getting the words right."

A. E. Housman

I do not choose the right word. I get rid of the wrong one.

Larry L. King

I work on each sentence until I'm satisfied with it and go on. I may rewrite one sentence nineteen times, and the next sentence eight times, and the next sentence three times. When I'm lucky, one sentence just once.

Helen MacInnes

With [*The Venetian Affair*] I went through three 500-sheet packages of the yellow paper and thirty or more soft black lead pencils. I used all 1,500 sheets but ended up with less than 500 pencil pages, so I guess I did constant rewriting as I went along.

Bernard Malamud

First drafts are for learning what your novel or story is about. Revision is working with that knowledge to enlarge and enhance an idea, to re-form it. D. H. Lawrence, for instance, did seven or eight drafts of *The Rainbow.* The first draft of a book is the most uncertain—where you need guts, the ability to accept the imperfect until it is better. Revision is one of the true pleasures of writing.

*

I work with language. I love the flowers of afterthought.

David Mamet

Write it out as verbose as you want. Have verbal Diarrhea. Then cut the unnecessary words, but keep the plot. Then rewrite and cut again. Then rewrite and cut *again.* After three times, you have something.

Richard Marius

I write through one draft [of fiction] to get to know my characters, to think about them, to wonder what they might do to reveal themselves first to me and then to readers. And when I am done with that draft, I love to start all over again, putting my new knowledge to work in the new version. The point is that revising time is thinking time, and the more thought you can pour into your writing, the better that writing is likely to be as long as you do not inflate the form until it loses its design.

William Maxwell

I revise, revise and revise so much, that by the time I've finished, I'm fairly secure in what I've done. . . . When it came time to go through the novel for the last time, when all the material was there, it was a matter of sticking to the tone, taking out what was pokey and slow. Doing that is rapture.

Phyllis McGinley

There *is* such a thing as inspiration (lower case) but it is no miracle. It is the reward handed to a writer for hard work and good conduct. It is the felicitous word sliding, after hours of evasion, obediently into place. It is a sudden comprehension of how to manufacture an effect, finish off a line or a stanza. At the triumphant moment this gift may seem like magic but actually it is the result of effort, practice, and the slight temperature a sulky brain is apt to run when it is pushed beyond its usual exertions.

Larry McMurtry

I normally do three drafts, never more and seldom less. The first draft is long and kind of an exploratory draft, with a lot of guesswork involved in it, some of it unsuccessful guesswork. Frequently in the first draft of a book there will be an element of redundancy, and you will write the same scene several times, an important scene in the novel, and you won't recognize perhaps you're doing that. The second draft is basically a cutting draft, in which you eliminate the bad guesses, pure mistakes, redundancies, and overwriting of all kinds. In the first draft when you're trying to develop a character, you let conversations run on for pages if you want to. In the second draft you tighten that. The third draft is stylistic basically. I don't pay much attention to style in the first two drafts; I write fairly rapidly, and I'm trying to visualize the scenes I'm describing as intensely as possible. The third draft is the stylist draft. I may get down to two eventually. I never want to go above three, because in a sense you participate in the emotions of the book every time you do a draft, and I think three times is about as many times as you can participate in those emotions and keep them alive. It goes cold.

Brian Moore

I do a great deal of rewriting. With the beginning of a book, I will often rewrite first paragraphs, and the first few pages, thirty and forty times, because another belief I have is that in that moment, in the fix, in those first crucial pages, all the reader's decisions are made.

Toni Morrison

Because the best part of all, the absolutely most delicious part, is finishing it and then doing it over. That's the thrill of a lifetime for me: if I can just get done with that first phase and then have infinite time to fix it and change it. I rewrite a lot, over and over again, so that it looks like I never did. I try to make it look like I never touched it, and that takes a lot of time and a lot of sweat.

Vladimir Nabokov

I have rewritten—often several times—every word I have ever published. My pencils outlast their erasers.

Joyce Carol Oates

The pleasure *is* the rewriting: The first sentence can't be written until the final sentence is written. This is a koan-like statement, and I don't mean to sound needlessly obscure or mysterious, but it's simply true. The completion of any work automatically necessitates its revisioning.

Cynthia Ozick

I scratch out a lot, and I never go on to the next sentence until the previous one is perfect. Then I type the manuscript and that's it. I never revise.

Nathalie Sarraute

I write a whole book from beginning to end—and then rewrite the text entirely, shaping it like poetry. This comes more easily, because there's a basis, while at the beginning one ventures into the void.

Anne Sexton

Like a surgeon, right down to the bone. That's why I liked it. My method in writing a poem is to expand, expand, and then slice, and then expand, then slice, then slice, cut. And that's the way it always works.

Irwin Shaw

There used to be only one sentence to write. You wrote it and it was good and you let it stay. As you grow older and more experienced you find that where you had one sentence before, you have thirty possibilities now and you have to stew to find the best.

Neil Simon

Rewriting is when playwriting really gets to be fun. In baseball you only get three swings and you're out. In rewriting, you get almost as many swings as you want and you know, sooner or later, you'll hit the ball.

Isaac Bashevis Singer

The main rule of a writer is never to pity your manuscript. If you see something is no good, throw it away and begin again. A lot of writers have failed because they have too much pity. They have already worked so much, they cannot just throw it away. But I say that the wastepaper basket is a writer's best friend. My wastepaper basket is on a steady diet.

Leo Tolstoy

I can't understand how anyone can write without rewriting anything over and over again. I scarely ever re-read my published writings, but if by chance I come across a page, it always strikes me: all this must be rewritten; this is how I should have written it. . . .

John Updike

Writing well involves two gifts—the art of adding and the art of taking away. Of the two, the first is more important, since without it the second could not exist.

Peter de Vries

When I see a paragraph shrinking under my eyes like a strip of bacon in a skillet, I know I'm on the right track.

Robert Penn Warren

I do think one thing is always true: the degree of self-criticism is only good for a veto. You can throw out what you've got wrong, and you can even try to say why it's wrong, but you can't say, "Now I am going to do it right."

H. G. Wells

No passion in the world is equal to the passion to alter someone else's draft.

Marguerite Yourcenar

On the third or fourth draft, pencil in hand, I reread my test, by this point practically a fair copy, and eliminate whatever can be eliminated, whatever seems useless. Each deletion is a triumph. At the bottom of every page I write, "crossed out seven words," "crossed out ten words," as the case may be. It gives me great pleasure to get rid of what is futile.

other quotations that help me write:

other quotations that help me write:

16

---

the feel
of writing

One of the reasons I collect and read quotations by writers on writing is companionship. I need to discover that other writers share my feelings at the writing desk. We are alone writing—and we want to be—but it helps to know what other writers are muttering to themselves while constructing their drafts.

The reader sees the final draft, neatly published, displaying all the fascistic authority of print. But the writer who produced that text was dealing in possibility, and all the what-might-be's had the same authority. It is exciting to write, in part because writing promises you large failures, terror, despair, exposure as well as the pleasure of making, discovering, learning, and being heard.

lost in the work

I have long known that I am as close to sanity as I will ever get when I am writing. If I were not a writer, I would have to find another activity in which I could lose myself.

I come to writing depressed, worried, angry, confused, fearful, unhappy, in pain, and, most of the time, I start a sentence and by the time I get to the end I am lost in the task. I forget the clock, do not realize the CD has played to the end, am not aware of the snow falling outside my window.

Writing brings one of the great gifts of life—a far greater gift than publication, applause, awards, even royalties—concentration. In the act of writing I experience a serene, quiet joy, a focus of all my energy and knowledge and craft on the task, losing myself in the job that strangely allows me to become myself.

I wish you the same gift.

Martin Amis

Writing a novel always feels to me like starting off in a very wide tunnel—in fact it doesn't look like a tunnel at all, since it's marvelously airy and free at the beginning, when you are assigning life to various propositions—but finishing off by crawling down a really cramped tunnel, because the novel has set up so many demands on you. There is so little room for manoeuvre by the end that you are actually a complete prisoner of the book, and it is formal demands that cause all those constrictions: the shape gets very tight by the end, and there are no choices any more.

W. H. Auden

When I'm writing a poem, most of the time I feel like a carpenter.

James Baldwin

You never get the book you wanted, you settle for the book you get.

Honoré de Balzac

I am a galley slave to pen and ink.

John Barth

There's a marine animal I'm fond of. (I don't think I invented him, though maybe I improved on him.) He's a crustacean who creates his spiral shell as he goes along. The materials he encounters are assimilated into it, and at the same time he more or less intuitively directs his path toward the kinds of material shells are best made of. How I love that animal! He's the perfect image for me. He moves at a snail's pace (and I do, too). He wears his history on his back all the time, but it's not just a burden; he's living in it. His history is his house. He's constantly adding new spirals, new rings—but they're not just repetition, for he's expanding logarithmically. Its volume becomes more capacious as new material is added from the present.

Marvin Bell

I can't go very long without writing and not become crabby, hard to live with. I always feel better when I write, when I go to my study out back under the wild cherry tree. It only takes a few minutes before I say, "Why didn't I come out here sooner?" It feels wonderful.

Truman Capote

One day I started writing, not knowing that I had chained myself for life to a novel but merciless master. When God hands you a gift, he also hands you a whip.

It was a lot of fun—at first. It stopped being fun when I discovered the difference between good writing and bad, and then came an even more terrifying discovery—the difference between very good writing and true art: it is subtle, but savage.

Geoffrey Chaucer
The lyf so short, the craft so long to lerne.

John Cheever
One never puts down a sentence without the feeling that it has never been put down in such a way, and that perhaps even the substance of the sentence has never been felt. Every sentence is an innovation.

Anton Chekhov
I wrote serenely, as if eating *bliny*.

Agatha Christie
[I'm] a sausage machine, a perfect machine.

Winston Churchill
Writing is an adventure. To begin with, it is a toy and an amusement. Then it becomes a mistress, then it becomes a master, then it becomes a tyrant. The last phase is that just as you are about to be reconciled to your servitude, you kill the monster and fling him to the public.

Joseph Conrad
I sit here religiously every morning—I sit down for eight hours every day—and the sitting down is all. In the course of that working say of 8 hours I write 3 sentences which I erase before leaving the table in despair. . . . Sometimes it takes all my resolution and power of self-control to refrain from butting my head against the wall.

Joan Didion
There is always a point in writing a piece when I sit in a room literally papered with false starts and cannot put one word after another and imagine that I have suffered a small stroke, leaving me apparently undamaged but actually aphasic.

Annie Dillard
One of the few things I know about writing is this: spend it all, shoot it, play it, lose it, all, right away, every time. Do not hoard what seems good for a later place in the book, or for another book; give it, give it all, give it now. The impulse to save something good for a better place later is the signal to spend it now. Something more will arise for later, something better. These things fill from behind, from beneath, like well water.

Lawrence Durrell

I feel like one of those machines for distilled water—it is coming drop by drop.

*

Miller toiled away like a monk, cleaning the keys and cogs of his typewriter every morning before sitting down to work: like a paid assassin checking and oiling his gun.

Jonathan Gash

I don't understand the seriousness with which some writers approach their work. . . . for me there is a necessity to regard writing as a game. I need it. It's a relief from my medical work. I try to pinch an hour or two whenever I can. It's play. And it's self-delighting.

Ellen Glasgow

I suppose I am a born novelist, for the things I imagine are more vital and vivid to me than the things I remember.

Gail Godwin

Once I begin the act of writing, it all falls away—the view from the window, the tools, the talismans, even the snoring cat—and I am unconscious of myself and my surroundings while I fuse language with idea, make a specific image visible or audible through the discovery of the right words. I can't describe the core of the writing experience because it really does occur in a sort of trance. One's carping inner critics are silenced for a time, and, as a result, what is produced is a little bit different from anything I had planned. There is always a surprise, a revelation. During the act of writing I have told myself something that I didn't know I knew.

Mary Gordon

Writing is an odd thing to do. You turn your back on the real world and favor an invisible world you invent. You have to search deep in your inner life. I hear things in a kinesthetic way. I tap into a rhythm of language to portray what I feel.

Donald Hall

The pleasure of writing is that the mind does not wander, anymore than it does in orgasm—and writing takes longer than orgasm. I can't stand movies because I cannot pay close continual attention. While I watch baseball I read a volume of letters between pitches. Even reading a good book—which is the third best thing—my mind sometimes wanders; or I watch myself reading. When I write I *never* watch myself writing; I only *am* the struggle to find or make the words.

Seamus Heaney

Of course, the reward of finishing the thing is pre-eminent still, perhaps
. . . but it's much challenged by the actual pleasure of feeling something
under your hand and growing.

Joseph Heller

It's not easy. But it's exciting, it's stimulating. If it were easy I wouldn't
want to do it.

John Hersey

When the writing is really working, I think there is something like
dreaming going on. I don't know how to draw the line between the
conscious management of what you're doing and this state. It usually
takes place in the earlier stages, in the drafting process. I would say that
it's related to day-dreaming. When I feel really engaged with a passage,
I become so lost in it that I'm unaware of my real surroundings, totally
involved in the pictures and sounds that that passage evokes.

John Hollander

A long project is like a secret houseguest, hidden in your study, waiting
to be fed and visited.

Paul Horgan

Preparation for the morning's task gets under way in an induced and
protracted absent-mindedness, as if to allow the work in progress to
come clear gradually, so that its daily rebirth suffers no jarring collision
with immediate reality, but establishes its own inner reality from which
it will draw conviction. Absurd as it may appear to those in other voca-
tions, any contact with a serious distraction, or obligation elsewhere,
may, at this daily moment, disturb a balance already delicate. A phone
call is a minor catastrophe and a knock on a door a potential disaster.
Until the day's work can actually begin, a frowning selfishness protects
all the ingredients of plan, design, idea, and will; and when it begins, it
flows forth, if the day is a good one, or it struggles forth if it is a poor
one; but strangely, later, it is difficult to tell by the evidence which pages
come from fluent work and which from halting . . . it is in this habit of
work where the writer finds his real sense of achievement—his very
content. He is really himself, at his best, only when he is observing his
rhythm of work.

A. E. Housman

Experience has taught me, when I am shaving of a morning, to keep
watch over my thoughts, because, if a line of poetry strays into my
memory, my skin bristles so that the razor ceases to act.

Job

Oh, that my words were now written. Oh, that they were printed in a book.

Franz Kafka

Art for the artist is only suffering, through which he releases himself for further suffering.

Robert Kelly

Craft is perfected attention.

William Kennedy

I love writing. I couldn't see any other life for me. I love words. The act of writing, in itself, is a pleasure.

Gunter Kunert

All I could do was to dangle from a fine thread of my own spinning over each day's abysses.

David Leavitt

I find that something almost magical happens when I put my fingers to the keyboard. I might walk around for days planning out scenes. But when you actually, physically, start to write, start putting words down, something different happens. A different part of your brain takes over and the results are often surprising and amazing.

Denise Levertov

You cannot will it to happen. But you can place yourself in a relationship to your art to be able to receive it if it should happen; this relationship is faithful attention.

Norman Mailer

Writers spend many hours alone, speaking to no one; they tend to draw on themselves, like drawing on a battery. One problem is to keep restoring one's ability to write and to keep the need to write live. It's like personal stripmining, and it takes a long time to recover.

Bernard Malamud

If it is winter in the book, spring surprises me when I look up.

Thomas Mann

A writer is a person for whom writing is more difficult than it is for other people.

Gabriel García Márquez

But when I sit down to write, which is the essential moment in my life, I am completely alone. Nobody can help me. Nobody knows exactly what I want to do—and sometimes I don't even know. I can't ask for help. It's total solitude.

Somerset Maugham

The author does not only write when he's at his desk, he writes all day long, when he is thinking, when he is reading, when he is experiencing; everything he sees and feels is significant to his purpose and, consciously or unconsciously, he is forever storing and making over his impressions.

Mekeel McBride

I know so many writers who think that life is tragic and that only tragic life can produce great art. I think that's bullshit. I think some people use writing as an excuse to live painful, complicated lives. I'm happy when I'm writing. That's why I do it. Some writers feel good ONLY when they're writing. When they're not writing, their lives are misery. That's not true for me. I can't stand that business about no writing, no life. There are lots of things I'd spend more time doing if I weren't writing. I'd paint. I'd quilt. I'd learn to play the harmonica and cane chairs.

John McPhee

The ultimate confrontation is with that blank sheet of paper.

When you're faced with that blank paper, all excuses are gone. The thing has to be written. I pace, I drink tea, I stare out the window and feel generally miserable. No, it would be absurd to give the impression of my methods as a kind of writing machine. If it is a machine, it's a lousy one. Sometimes I go to that office and nothing happens all day, nothing, for 12 hours.

*

Writing is a suspension of life in order to re-create life.

Medieval Scribe

Three fingers hold the pen, but the whole body toils.

Arthur Miller

Writing is hard work. It's like being in a dark cave. You don't know where the walls are, the boundaries of the play. You have to sense the limits of where you are, what you're doing and where you're going.

Toni Morrison

I *can* concentrate. When I sit down to write I never brood. I have so many other things to do, with *my* children and teaching, that I can't afford it. I brood, think of ideas, in the automobile when I'm driving to work or in the subway or when I'm mowing the lawn. By the time I get to the paper something's there—I can produce.

Joyce Carol Oates

My life is sort of double narrative, *my* life running alongside an interior/fictional life.

Flannery O'Connor

I never completely forget myself except when I am writing and I am never more completely myself than when I am writing.

Jayne Anne Phillips

Real writers serve their material. They allow it to pass through them and have the opportunity to move beyond the daily limitations of being inside themselves. It's like being led by a whisper.

Marge Piercy

Good work habits are nothing more than habits that let you work, that encourage you to pay attention. Focus is most of it: to be fierce and pointed, so that everything else momentarily sloughs away.

Sylvia Plath

Nothing stinks like a pile of unpublished writing.

Philip Roth

You have to gut a book through.

Georges Simenon

I am an artisan; I need to work with my hands. I would like to carve my novels in a piece of wood.

Red Smith

There's nothing to writing. All you do is sit down at the typewriter and open a vein.

Stephen Spender

The problem of creative writing is essentially one of concentration, and the supposed eccentricities of poets are usually due to mechanical habits or rituals developed in order to concentrate. Concentration, of course,

for the purposes of writing poetry, is different from the kind of concentration required for working out a sum. It is a focusing of the attention
in a special way, so that the poet is aware of all the implications and
possible developments of his idea, just as one might say that a plant was
not concentrating on developing mechanically in one direction, but in
many directions, towards the warmth and light with its leaves, and
towards the water with its roots, all at the same time.

William Stafford

I feel like a surf rider in the language; the luck involved is at least equal
to any skill. I find myself being taken for a ride, and the ride always
goes further than I thought I could go.

David Storey

It's like working in a coal mine. I sit down to eight hours of slog a day
and do a kind of shift of prose.

Henry David Thoreau

Time never passes so quickly and unaccountably as when I am engaged
in compostion, i.e. in writing down my thoughts. Clocks seem to have
been put forward.

Leo Tolstoy

. . . talent, which consists in the capacity to direct intense concentrated
attention.

*

One ought to write when one leaves a piece of one's flesh in the inkpot
each time one dips one's pen.

Paul Valéry

A poem is never finished, only abandoned.

Peter de Vries

I love being a writer. What I can't stand is the paperwork.

Robert Penn Warren

I found it a lonely life, trying to write. It seemed to set one apart from
life, to be, as it were, a sort of mystic deprivation, to create what can
only be described as a psychic void that needed to be filled. Sometimes,
paradoxically, it was as though the only way to be not lonely was to
be alone.

other quotations that help me write:

bibliography

for further reading

In keeping with the tone of *Shoptalk*, this is a personal reading list, not a scholarly bibliography. These are some of the books on my shelves that have been my companions at the writing desk, books that have made me feel that I am part of a community of writers. I have annotated the list to help you find books that will allow you to talk with fellow writers. I have emphasized collections of interviews with writers since this is the resource least utilized in the academy.

Any such list will be controversial. There are books left off that I might add tomorrow and others on the list I might drop tomorrow. You will know of books not on my list that you think should be, and I hope you will discover others that you'll want to add. Many of these books made a difference for me at a crucial time in my writing life, and their citations reflect an emotional commitment as much as an intellectual one. I have listed only a few of the thousands I have read—and also bought—over the fifty years of my continuing apprenticeship to the trade of writer.

The single most important source is *Writers at Work—the Paris Review Interviews*. This is the place to start. All eight books are in print in hardcover by Viking and paper by Penguin. And each issue of the *Paris Review* includes new interviews.

The University of Michigan publishes an extensive and extraordinary series of books under the general title of *Poets on Poetry;* each focuses on an individual poet and includes interviews, statements, and essays with and by the poet. The University of Mississippi has a similar series that is not limited to a single genre. As soon as you start to read in this area, you will discover the extraordinary availability of material by writers on how and why they write.

Some of my other favorite books are:

• Allen, Walter, ed. *Writers on Writing*. New York: Dutton, 1959; Boston: The Writer, 1988.

> *The collection that made me realize the extent and richness of the material available. My copy is marked and remarked on almost every page.*

- Allott, Miriam. *Novelists on the Novel.* New York: Columbia University Press, 1959, o.p.
- Bowen, Catherine Drinker. *Adventures of a Biographer.* Boston: Little, Brown, 1959, o.p.
- Dillard, Annie. *The Writing Life.* New York: Harper and Row, 1989.
- Faulkner, William. *Faulkner in the University: Class Conferences at the University of Virginia, 1957-58.* Edited by Frederick L. Gwynn and Joseph L. Blotner. New York: Random House, Vintage Books, 1965; facsimile of 1959 edition available from University of Virginia Press, Charlottesville, Virginia.
- Funke, Lewis. *Playwrights Talk About Writing.* Chicago: Dramatic Publishing Co., 1975, o.p.
- Greene, Graham. *In Search of a Character: Two African Journals.* New York: Viking, 1962; Penguin, 1981.
- Hale, Nancy. *The Realities of Fiction: A Book About Writing.* Boston: Little, Brown, 1962; Westport, CT: Greenwood, 1977.
- Hersey, John. *The Writer's Craft.* New York: Random House, 1973.
- Horgan, Paul. *Approaches to Writing: Reflections and Notes on the Art of Writing from a Career of Half a Century.* New York: Farrar, Straus & Giroux, 1973; Middletown, CT: Wesleyan University Press, 1988.
- Mann, Thomas. *The Story of a Novel: The Genesis of "Dr. Faustus".* New York: Knopf, 1961, o.p.
- McCormack, Thomas, ed. *Afterwords: Novelists on Their Novels.* New York: Harper and Row, 1969; St. Martins, 1988.
- McPhee, John. *The John McPhee Reader.* Edited by William Howarth. New York: Random House, Vintage Books, 1976.
  > *The preface to this book reveals, in exceptional detail, the fascinating reporting and writing process of an outstanding nonfiction writer.*
- Packard, William, ed. *The Craft of Poetry: Interviews from "The New York Quarterly."* Garden City, NJ: Doubleday, 1974; New York: Paragon House, 1987.
- Steegmuller, Francis. *Flaubert and Madame Bovary: A Double Portrait.* New York: Random House, Vintage Books, 1939, 1950; Chicago: University of Chicago Press, 1977.
  > *An absolutely astonishing biography of the making of one of the most influential novels in our literary history.*
- Sternburg, Janet, ed. *The Writer on Her Work.* New York: Norton, 1981.
  > *If I had to pick one book on this list, Sternburg's would be it.*
- Trask, Georgianne, and Burkhart, Charles, eds. *Storytellers and Their Art.* Garden City, NJ: Doubleday, Anchor, 1963, o.p.

- Webber, Jeanette L., and Grumman, Joan, eds. *Woman as Writer.* Boston: Houghton Mifflin, 1978.
- Welty, Eudora. *One Writer's Beginnings.* Cambridge: Harvard University Press, 1984; New York: Warner Books, 1985.
- Winokur, Jon, ed. *Writers on Writing.* Philadelphia: Running Press, 1986.

index

index of quotations by author